Vatican II

A Universal Call to Holiness

EDITED BY
Anthony J. Ciorra
AND
Michael W. Higgins

PAULIST PRESS
New York / Mahwah, NJ

Except as otherwise noted, all translations of the sixteen Vatican II documents are taken from www.vatican.va. Except as otherwise noted, all translations of the closing addresses comprising the starting points for each essay are taken from Walter M. Abbott, ed., *The Documents of Vatican II* (New York: The America Press, 1966).

Cover design by Sharyn Banks
Book design by Lynn Else

ISBN 978-0-8091-4787-8

Library of Congress Control Number: 2012946895

Published by Paulist Press
997 Macarthur Boulevard
Mahwah, New Jersey 07430

www.paulistpress.com

Printed and bound in the
United States of America

Contents

Introduction

Anthony J. Ciorra

Yves Congar, OP, a *peritus* at the Second Vatican Council, wrote an important essay about the importance of the Council entitled "The Council as an Assembly and the Church as Essentially Conciliar." The Conference celebrating the fiftieth anniversary of the Second Vatican Council sponsored by Sacred Heart University and Paulist Press on April 23–24, 2012, in Fairfield, Connecticut, did exactly what Congar proposed in his essay. People gathered from throughout the United States, Canada, and China to celebrate the most important event in the Catholic Church in four hundred years. The group became an assembly that listened carefully, engaged in conversation and responded creatively. The church that gathered in Fairfield, Connecticut, was an *ecclesia discerns*, a learning church.

Pope John XXIII announced the Second Vatican Council on January 25, 1959. He presided at the opening of the Council on October 11, 1962, and Paul VI celebrated its conclusion on December 8, 1965. This was the largest and most diverse gathering of the Church in its entire history. There were 2500 bishops, theologians, observers, and representatives from other Christian and non-Christian religions. There were 116 countries represented at the Council as compared to the First Vatican Council where 40 percent of the bishops present were from Italy. At the time of the First Vatican Council, the missionary bishops were of European origin since there was not yet an indigenous episcopate throughout the world. The Second Vatican Council was for the first time a council of the world Church.

The Council was about relationships among diverse cultures, theological viewpoints, and multiple religious traditions. The Vatican II Conference in Connecticut emerged from a relationship between Sacred Heart University and Paulist Press. Sacred Heart

1

Introduction

University was conceived as the result of the Second Vatican Council. Bishop Walter Curtis was the Bishop of Bridgeport when Pope John called the Council. He attended all of the sessions of the Council. He was passionate about the vision of the Council and worked tirelessly to implement its sixteen documents in the diocese. Because he was especially moved by the "Decree on the Apostolate of the Laity," he founded Sacred Heart University in 1963 as the first lay-led university in the United States.

Paulist Press shaped its mission and flourished as a result of the Second Vatican Council. The Press was committed to producing cutting-edge works about the Council to educate and inspire the American Church to implement its vision. The success of the reception of the Council in the United States was due in no small measure to Paulist Press and its publications.

There was an obvious synergy between the Paulist Press and Sacred Heart University because of the Second Vatican Council. The relationship that evolved between members of these two institutions engendered the Vatican II Fiftieth Anniversary Celebration Conference, "Universal Call to Holiness." The planning committee had many lively conversations about the meaning of the Council and its importance for the twenty-first century.

The consensus among the planners was that the statement about the universal call to holiness was the watershed moment at the Second Vatican Council. The Council Fathers began their discussion on holiness within the context of the "Decree on the Appropriate Renewal of the Religious Life." After much debate and discussion, the fathers moved the call to holiness to the "Dogmatic Constitution on the Church" (*Lumen Gentium*):

> The followers of Christ, called by God, not in virtue of their works but by the design of grace, and justified in the Lord Jesus, have been made sons of God in the baptism of faith and partakers- of the divine nature, and so are truly sanctified.... It is therefore quite clear that all Christians in any state or walk of life are called to the fullness of Christian life and to the perfection of love, and by this holiness a more human manner of life is fostered also in earthly society....Therefore all the faithful

are invited and obliged to holiness and the perfection of their own state of life.[1]

In the Hebrew Scriptures, to be in the presence of the holy was often a shattering and terrifying experience. At different times in Israel's history, holiness was reduced to external practices. The Israelites saw themselves as holy, as being set apart. Both the Hebrew word for "holiness," *qds*, and the Greek word *hagos* mean "to set apart." The incarnation gave new meaning to holiness. The God who became human was not set apart but rather came in the flesh to teach us that holiness was about becoming human.

The Second Vatican Council was incarnational in its theology. It was a pastoral council that was concerned about the needs of the human family. The universal call to holiness comes from its theological vision. Baptism is the hermeneutic for understanding the Council's emphasis on holiness. The Council not only recaptured the importance of baptism but also gave it prominence as the single event that calls all women and men to holiness. The two Council documents that laid the foundation for a contemporary understanding of holiness are the "Decree on the Apostolate of the Laity," and "The Pastoral Constitution on the Church in the Modern World" (*Gaudium et Spes*).

Two new doors were opened as a result of these documents. The door of ministry was opened for laity because of their baptismal call. The laity are at the heart of the Church by the mere fact that they comprise ninety-nine percent of the Catholic faith . In fact, it was John Henry Newman who once said "The Church would look very foolish without them. "The second door that was opened was the one to the world. The Council decreed in the "Pastoral Constitution on the Church in the Modern World" (*Gaudium et Spes*):

> The joys and the hopes, the griefs and the anxieties of the men of this age, especially those who are poor or in any way afflicted, these too are the joys and hopes, the griefs and anxieties of the followers of Christ. Indeed, nothing genuinely human fails to raise an echo in their hearts.... That is why this community realizes that it is truly and

intimately linked with mankind and its history....Hence this Second Vatican Council...now addresses itself without hesitation not only...to the Church...but to the whole of humanity.[2]

The recovery of the centrality of baptism called all to holiness and ministry. *Gaudium et Spes* placed the mission of the baptized in the world. The Council thus adapted the new way of holiness in the world that Jesus modeled for us.

The spirit of the Council was just as important as its content. The Council Fathers wrestled with the relationship of three important issues: faith and modern science, the Church and the modern state, and Christianity and other religions. In effect, the Council was engaging with the world. The style in dealing with these issues was one of open debate and discussion. The Council Fathers embraced the tension of multiple viewpoints that required heroic charity to move beyond ideological positions. The style of the Council documents was inspirational and invitational. John O'Malley summarizes the change in style that took place at the Council.

> I will summarize in a simple litany some of the elements in the change in style of the Church indicated by the council's vocabulary: from commands to invitations, from laws to ideals, from threats to persuasion, from coercion to conscience, from monologue to conversation, from ruling to serving, from withdrawn to integrated, from vertical and top-down to horizontal, from exclusion to inclusion, from hostility to friendship, from static to changing, from passive acceptance to active engagement, from prescriptive to principled, from defined to open-ended, from behavior-modification to conversion of heart, from the dictates of the law to the dictates of conscience, from external conformity to the joyful pursuit of holiness.[3]

The shift in style is a paradigm shift for the Roman Catholic culture. O'Malley would hold that this represents a new model of spirituality. It was precisely this style and spirit that the Vatican II

Conference at Sacred Heart University wanted to recapture, not only for the conference but also as a reminder of what we as Church are called to be in the twenty-first century.

It was for this reason that the planning committee decided to create a conference that would be poetic rather than prosaic. Rather than engaging in a review and critique of the sixteen Council documents, we decided to pick up where the Council left off. When the Council concluded on December 8, 1965, seven brief speeches were given by cardinals selected from the four corners of the universe. Pope Paul VI introduced the seven speeches in this way:

> For the Catholic Church, no one is a stranger. No one is excluded. No one is far away. Everyone to whom our greeting is addressed is one who is called, who is invited and who, in a certain sense is present. This is the language of the heart of one who loves. Every loved one is present. Behold this is our greeting. May it rise as a new spark of divine charity in our hearts, a spark which may enkindle the principles, doctrine and proposals which the council has organized and which, thus inflamed by charity, may really produce in the Church and in the world that renewal of thoughts, activities, conduct, moral force and hope and joy which was the very scope of the council.[4]

The seven speeches that followed were addressed to: Rulers; Men of Thought and Science; Artists; Women; the Poor, the Sick, and the Suffering; Workers; and Youth. These speeches are not exhaustive presentations, nor are they literary masterpieces. They are an example of the pastoral style and vision of the Council. The implementation of the Council's directives and principles was being passed on to these seven constituencies in the Church and the world. The purpose of the Vatican II Conference was to harness the energy of the Council for the agenda of the twenty-first century.

The opening address at the Conference, "The Future of Vatican II: The Vision of the Council beyond the Narratives" by Dr. Massimo Faggioli, set the historical context and principles for the accurate interpretation of the Council. The seven presentations

The Future of Vatican II

Looking at Vatican II and its message for the Church today means looking at the history not only of the Council itself but also of its reception and interpretation in these last fifty years.[2] The texts of Vatican II would not survive out of the fertile ground of theological and pastoral reflection on those very texts. As Bernard Häring said about the last day of Vatican II, December 8, 1965, "the council begins today."[3] That was true for December 8, 1965, the last day of Vatican II, as it is for every day.

That is why is not surprising—actually, it is reassuring—to look at the early history of post–Vatican II and see that there was, and very early on, an interruption between the enthusiasm of the celebration of the final days of Vatican II and the first steps of its reception and interpretation.[4] In a way, the naïve enthusiasm for a supposedly easy "fresh start" for Catholicism had long disappeared, even before the conclusion of the Council in 1965. As Yves Congar wrote in the very first page of his Council diary written the first day after Vatican II, December 9, 1965 (my translation): "What a desk! I have stacks of books and journals everywhere: on the table, on the chairs, on the floor! What a job!!!"[5] He was just talking about his desk, but in a way he was talking also about the agenda of the Catholic Church after Vatican II already.

The first few years of the age of Vatican II

For some historians of the post–Vatican II era the age of "euphoria" lasted only ten years, until 1975, followed by a decade of "contestations," and then concluded by the current period of *"restauration"* that had begun well before 2005.[6] For some others the "honeymoon" between Vatican II and the world *ad extra* had ended already in 1968, the peak of the sixties, at least in the Western hemisphere: the student protest movements, the counter-culture, and the rise of political violence.[7]

But also from an intra-Catholic perspective, it can be argued that the honeymoon between the Council, the pope, and main-stream culture lasted even less than ten years. The first celebration of the newly created Bishops' Synod came in 1967; before the second session of the Synod could gather in 1969, during the summer of 1968, Paul VI's encyclical *Humanae Vitae* had become the symbol of the first crisis in the renewed relationship between Church and modern world.[8] It became clear that the interpretation of Vatican II would be touched by the new emphasis of modern Catholicism on moral issues.[9]

All that said, and no matter what our periodization is, it is undeniable that at the beginning of the 1970s Vatican II had already become the underlying platform for the renewal of Catholicism in different fields: liturgy, biblical studies, ecclesiology, ecumenism and interreligious dialog. Changes in Catholic theology also entailed changes in the structure of the Catholic Church—or this is what many thought at the time.[10] The seventies were the first—and so far the last—decade of cautious decentralization of Roman Catholicism:[11] decentralization of the balance of power in the Church as an institution, and displacement of the centers where Catholic theology was thought, taught, and lived.[12]

The clash with the Lefebvrian schism made clear already in the mid-1970s that Catholic theology was not to be reduced to nostalgia for a historically determined political and social ideology of European Catholicism—often bordering with the political worldview of fascism and with the conspiracy mindset including anti-Semitism and theological anti-Judaism.[13] With the first pope of the post-conciliar period (the same pope who brought the Council to a conclusion), Paul VI, Vatican II experienced its first decade of reform, renewal, and experiments.

But failure and disappointments have strangely become, in the eyes of many, more visible than the many successes of the council. Vatican II seems subject to a midlife crisis: today, when Catholics and theologians form their judgment about Vatican II the risk is to focus more on the failures than on the successes. It is also true that in some quarters of neo-conservative Catholicism failures have become more important and cherished than successes. But Church historians know how the Council of Trent was talked about after fifty years from its conclusion: the state of the reception of Vatican II is now, at fifty years of age, certainly not worse than the application of the Council of Trent at the beginning of the seventeenth century.[14]

That is why no matter how successful these reforms and experiments were, Pope Paul VI has become, especially for the ultra-nostalgic and ultra-conservative fringe of Catholicism, the uncomfortable paradigm of a "reformist pope,"[15] if not (as Paul VI is for the Lefebvrites) the bogeyman of Catholicism facing modernity. The historiographical and theological silence about Giovanni Battista Montini—Paul VI (just like the silence about John XXIII, except for a few specialists of Vatican II)—is a very clear sign of the theological *Zeitgeist* in the Catholic Church of today. This harsh judgment on the popes of Vatican II involves and assumes for some an even harsher judgment on the Council that they announced in 1959 and led until its end in 1965.

From John Paul II to Benedict XVI

A new phase in the reception of Vatican II began in 1978 with the election of John Paul II, the last pope who had been a Council father of Vatican II. The caution of Catholic theologians in assessing John Paul II's legacy regarding the reception of Vatican II has today more to do with the fear of fueling the ongoing neo-conservative backlash than with the length and complexity of his pontificate.[16] The difficult position of Vatican II theologians in assessing Wojtyla's contribution to the reception of Vatican II is now between the generous but often also confusing "conciliar nominalism" of John Paul II, and the active effort of reinterpretation of the Council in a minimizing way brought about by the Roman curia and the willing entourage of Pope Benedict XVI more than by Pope Benedict XVI himself.

It is undeniable that the vulgarized and tabloid-like propaganda about Pope Benedict XVI's interpretation of the Council lends itself perfectly to feed the theological side of the "culture wars," especially in the West and the North American continent. The phenomenon of political conversions to Catholicism in the North Atlantic scene (America and Europe) is not immune from this debate and does in fact influence it.[17]

For theological pundits and ultraconservative Catholic bloggers, the theology of Vatican II seems to function sometimes as collateral—an openly negotiable thing in the Church of the "non-negotiables"—not only for the relationships within the Church and its various souls but especially for relations with the various parties of nostalgia: for Lefebvrists as well as for converts who have chosen Catholicism as the home of choice for their neo-conservative worldview.[18] In this sense it is no coincidence that the focus of the interpretation of the Council during the pontificate of Pope Benedict XVI is clearly centered on "political-ecclesiastical considerations."[19]

Now, fifty years after the beginning of Vatican II, in some Catholic quarters there is a sense of disappointment for the failed promises of the Church and of the Council. The historiographical work on the Council tells us that this disappointment is related to the vast underestimation among Council Fathers and theologians active at the Council of the work that needed to be done *after* its conclusion. On the other hand, what seems to be the prevalent sentiment—a parallel to the underestimation of the first generation—is an underestimation of the work *already done* by the Council for the renewal of Catholicism. The simple fact that the Catholic Church cannot simply understand itself and present itself to the world of today without Vatican II was made evident in the controversial lifting of the excommunications of the Lefebvrite bishops in January 2009, the fiftieth anniversary of the announcement of the Council.[20]

The coincidence of that anniversary in 2009 with the lifting of the excommunications of the four bishops ordained by Marcel Lefebvre has focused a new kind of attention on the Council and has created a situation that is leading to a new understanding of its significance. The debate on the meaning of the Council entered a new stage there. Not only have bishops' conferences and individual bishops spoken out, and, understandably, representatives of Jewish communities around the world but also political leaders in parliaments and similar bodies have done so, even if sometimes discreetly. Their reactions have forced the Holy See to acknowledge the central point at issue: the meaning of Vatican II. This is because the followers of Lefebvre have proclaimed from the beginning their refusal to accept the Council and particularly to accept certain elements of its corpus. Their only reason for existence is their rejection of the Council.

In the horizon of the contemporary Church, contemporary politics, and international public opinion, the Second Vatican Council has shown itself to be a "guarantee of citizenship" for the of Vatican II.[25] The effort to form a vision becomes helpless when it is detached from an understanding of their historical developments. It is now time to offer here a few insights based on an inter-textual and intra-textual interpretation of the documents in light of the history of the event Vatican II.[26]

Vertical and horizontal in Vatican II

In a recent two-volume work, the German-French Jesuit Christoph Theobald has described the documents of Vatican II as bi-directional: a vertical axis and a horizontal axis that fundamentally represent the overall vision of the Council.[27] The major documents of Vatican II all have both a vertical or spiritual dimension and a horizontal or social dimension. But some of the final documents have the function to expand the global message of the Council in one direction or the other.

The key documents building the vertical axis are the constitution on the Revelation *Dei Verbum*, the pastoral constitution *Gaudium et Spes*, and the declaration on religious freedom, *Dignitatis Humanae*. Thanks to these three documents, says Theobald, the Church can once again "have access to the source," that is, the revelation in God's word. In this sense the vision of Vatican II is essentially *ressourcement*, the quest for a new access to the same source but after a hermeneutical reframing (*recadrage*) of Catholic theology in light of a Church in transition from its European and Western paradigm toward the paradigm of a world or global Catholicism, after the first transition from Christianity as a Jewish religion to a hellenistic-mediterranean religion in the first centuries. The vertical axis of the vision of Vatican II cannot survive without a deep understanding of the new cultural geography of Catholicism. Vatican II, the first global-ecumenical council, assumes this new paradigm starting from the very identity of its participants.

The vertical axis means, for the access to the Bible and the tradition, a new emphasis from "revelation as instruction" to "revelation as communication," the involvement of all the Church members in bringing the Scripture into the life of the Church, and a necessary role of reception also for the *paradosis* of the Scripture. The same vertical axis means, for the relationship between Church and world, an acute awareness of the signs of the times and the need for the Church and for every Christian to discern and to make a decision, thus calling every Christian to the need to look at the climates he/she lives in, and to seek truth as the reason for the right to religious freedom in light of the revelation.

The second dimension is the horizontal axis built by the Council documents. This horizontal dimension gives foundation to the reframing operated by Vatican II and that constitutes the vision of Vatican II as a new relational understanding of the Church. This relational dimension of the Church grounds the ecclesiology of Vatican II after the era of apologetics and of hierarchical idolatry or—in Yves Congar's words—"hierarchology" (*Lumen Gentium*), builds the pastoral and missionary dimension of the Church (*Gaudium et Spes* and *Ad Gentes*), its ecumenical and interreligious dimensions (*Unitatis Redintegratio* and *Nostra Aetate*), and the liturgy according to *Sacrosanctum Concilium* as the center of Christian life and of the Church in its local realization. Communication with God is nothing if it is not reflected in a human way of communicating and relating horizontally. The two ecclesiological constitutions and *Nostra Aetate* give theological expression to this horizontal orientation: ecumenism, interreligious relations, the Old Testament and the relations with the Jews, atheism, and modern culture.

For Theobald the vertical and the horizontal dimension of the Council documents meet in the ecclesiology of Vatican II, and especially in *Lumen Gentium*. Mission and conversion of the Church in the pilgrimage of the people of God does not identify itself statically with the Church of Christ, but needs constant reform (the *subsistit in* of *Lumen gentium* 8). Ecumenical dimension, institutional framework of the Church, and its eschatological orientation lived in the liturgy build the connection between the two axes.[28]

Ressourcement *and* rapprochement

Crossing the paths of the different council documents we can identify another couple of ideas that are crucial and common to the message of Vatican II: *ressourcement* and *rapprochement*.

The idea of *ressourcement* is at the heart of the constitutions on revelation and on liturgy. The idea of *ressourcement* drives Catholic theology to the rediscovery of the first source of the Christian message—Scripture—and of the early sources of an undivided Christianity: Tradition (with a capital *T*), the Fathers of the Church, and liturgy. *Ressourcement* wanted to give back to the Fathers of the Church the influence they had had in the education of the leadership of Catholicism and that was lost in favor of neo-Scholastic theology, and that also had become suspect of modernistic heresy at the beginning of the twentieth century.[29]

Ressourcement puts at the center of theology what needs to be at the center, and reorganizes everything else with a compass that uses the category of "historicity" in theology in order to make theology free from history and at the same time more faithful to a Tradition dynamically understood. The idea of development in theology thus finds itself not automatically excommunicated nor blessed, but examined in light of the coherence with the very sources of theology and its main operating principle, the pastoral character of the doctrine *salus animarum*, the salvation of the souls.

In this sense, Vatican II is an event not only for what it accomplished, but also for what it did decide to reject. For example, the Council Fathers did not accept the early proposals coming from some European bishops aiming at giving Catholics not the Bible, but a purified and selective collection of biblical texts, an anthology with only selected and untroubling passages from a few books of the Bible. Vatican II decided not only to put the Scripture back into the hands of the faithful, but also to draw the epistemological consequences of this decision for the whole balance of Catholic theology.[30]

Liberating theology and the faithful from the shadow of the suspicion of anti-biblicism is today an almost forgotten fact, especially in European Catholicism, as is forgotten the accomplishment of the liturgical reform as the most important reform in Roman Catholicism in the last five centuries.[31] The idea of liturgy as a source for Christian theology and Christian life made that reform as important back then as it is controversial in some Catholic quarters. It is thus clear that belittling its accomplishments is possible only if we forget the role of liturgy in Catholic theology in the twentieth century, before the Council and after the Council.[32]

Secondly, the idea of *rapprochement* is at the core of the very idea of calling an ecumenical council after World War II. The watershed of the two world wars called Church leaders and theologians, very early on, to make a shift towards a theology and a Church that could contribute to the idea of a fundamental unity of human kind. One of the main aims of the council announced by John XXIII was to summon the Church and celebrate its unity in a new relationship with the outer world.[33] But Vatican II was meant to be a "celebration" in the most profound liturgical sense:[34] not a mere display of false unanimity, but a living experience of communion within the Church and with the world through the interaction of different cultural sensibilities, historical backgrounds, and theological orientations.

The liturgical movement and the theology of Vatican II reflected the impact of the dialogical principle in twentieth-century western philosophy: Husserl, Buber, Levinas, Gadamer.[35] The liturgical reform expressed the deep theological aspiration of the Church to shape itself in the form of Jesus as "the universal brother of all human beings" *("le Frère universel de tous les humains," "mort pour tous les hommes sans exception")* in the words of Charles de Foucauld (1858-1916), a French Catholic religious and priest living among the Tuareg in the Sahara desert in Algeria.

Vatican II continued the tradition of unity expressed through liturgy, but through an understanding of *rapprochement*—re-approaching, reaching out, and reconciliation—that expressed more clearly the attempt of Vatican II of making of the "Church a sacrament of reconciliation" for humankind.[36] The idea of *rapprochement*—a term used many times by the pioneer of ecumenism and liturgist Dom Lambert Beauduin[37]—is not part of the corpus of Vatican II in a material way, but it belongs fully to the aims of Vatican II. Rapprochement in the theology of Vatican II means seeking a new unity between peoples, nations, and cultures (in the constitution *Gaudium et Spes*), between different religions and faiths (in the declaration *Nostra aetate*), between Christian churches (in the decree on ecumenism *Unitatis redintegratio*), and within the Catholic Church (constitution on the liturgy *Sacrosanctum Concilium* and on the Church *Lumen Gentium*): above all, rapprochement with God through a renewed understanding and practice of the sacraments.[38] In John O'Malley's words, if the Church of Vatican II is visible through its new "style," much of its style is represented by rapprochement as the style of the Church,[39] as the end of the era of polemical apologetics as the only proof of catholicity.

Church and world in the twenty-first century

In evaluating the vision of Vatican II we must always consider the temptation to take one specific period of the history of the Church as the "golden age." On another anniversary of Vatican II, the twentieth anniversary in 1982, the theologian of the council Marie-Dominique Chenu, OP, reminded us: "Vatican II produced texts so rich that their application went necessarily beyond the letter of the texts."[40] This was true not only of Vatican II, but also of the Council of Trent, and reminds us that whatever the clash of interpretations about Vatican II will bring us, much of what Vatican II was has become reality in the Catholic Church. Much has been done; much still needs to be done; its major accomplishments cannot be undone anymore.

Vatican II and our age

For the few anti-Vatican II Catholics, the Council carries the guilt of having put to an end the "golden age" of a religion that in their mind was righteously and healthily reluctant to engage with modernity. The price for that golden age of intellectual stability and moral certainty was a sense of self-righteousness that came from a staunch opposition to a "world" metaphysically understood and seen as necessarily evil, though in a political and counter-revolutionary sense more than in a Paulinian understanding of the relationship between the Christian and the danger of "conforming to the mentality of this world" (Rom 12:2).

On the other side, in some quarters of more liberal Catholicism the simple mention of Vatican II triggers a "veterans' sentimentality," of the ones who were there or who had seen that moment, and think that it is gone. They feel that such a golden age was too brief and too good to last, and that it has been betrayed because this is what always happens in the Catholic Church. Their sociological approach to Vatican II as a purely cultural event sometimes takes for granted the theological value of the Council.

Both perspectives are not only too pessimistic: they also both miss one of the major points of Vatican II, which was exactly the rejection of the idea of a golden age in history. For all its theological appreciation of history and historicity as sources for theology, the only golden age Vatican II had in mind was the one of the Gospel, which we can approach theologically through *ressourcement.*

Fidelity to the Gospel, not to a golden age (whenever that age was) is one of the key ideas of the Council as an event of a world-church. This reorientation of Catholic theology entails a new relationship to the idea of culture, and makes of Vatican II a countercultural council: if only for the refusal of Catholicism either to reduce itself to a "culture" or to tie itself to a historically-connotated culture.[41]

This is what makes Vatican II a true compass (as it is written in the spiritual testament of John Paul II) for the future of the Church:

> As I stand on the threshold of the Third Millennium "in medio Ecclesiae," I would like once again to express my gratitude to the Holy Spirit for the great gift of the Second Vatican Council, to which, together with the whole Church—and especially with the whole Episcopate—I feel indebted. I am convinced that it will long be granted to the new generations to draw from the treasures that this 20th-century Council has lavished upon us. As a Bishop who took part in the Council from the first to the last day, I desire to entrust this great patrimony to all who are and will be called in the future to put it into practice.[42]

On a world map whose visible and invisible boundaries have significantly shifted in the last fifty years, Catholicism can call itself a world church because of its new freedom received by the council in terms of relationship between theology and cultures.

Vatican II and our church

The vision of Vatican II is crucial not only for the survival of the Church in the age of the culture wars, but also for the viability of theology in modernity. On one side, clearly long overdue were the shifts about biblical hermeneutic, theology and modern science, interreligious and the ecumenical dialog. On the other side, for other theological issues Vatican II opened a path towards the future of the Church: a more communional and less juridical ecclesiology, a new understanding of the relationship between laity and ministry, and Church reform.

It is thus clear that Vatican II was not only a "reform council," but also a "paradigmatic event" for the life of the Church and its inner vitality. The *aggiornamento* of Catholic theology represents still today an example of both courage and foresight, in the way these reforms were debated and decided. Vatican II is the latest, not the last, moment of representation of conciliarity in the Church and a testimony of the link between conciliarity and reform.[43]

With Vatican II and after Vatican II, the theological reflection has re-discovered *synodality* and *conciliarity* as basic features of Christianity, Catholicism included. The Council has once again demonstrated that nineteenth-century ultramontanism was a phenomenon typical of the siege mentality that shaped Catholicism in the "long nineteenth century," and that conciliarity and collegiality are processes, not just one-time events. Vatican II reminds us that councils and synods are the places and moments *par excellence* where Christian churches have reached an ecclesial consensus in matters of faith and discipline in particular moments of their history.[44]

Secondly, in its paradigmatic character, Vatican II is shaping Catholic theology so that theology after Vatican II need not limit itself to a "theology of the interpretation of Vatican II."[45] This is where the current battle fought in some quarters for the meaning of Vatican II reveals its futility. Vatican II is essential for the Church because the Council is not about itself, but rather is about re-centering theology in the very roots of the Christian revelation without losing sight of the signs of our times.

It is no surprise that many of the new features of the Catholic Church after Vatican II surpassed the letter of the Council documents: this is true both for the liberal and the conservative interpretation of the Council.[46] This also reveals one of the key aspects of the vision of Vatican II, the real common ground of Catholicism in an ideologically polarized era: the fundamental shift from a Church as an institution to a Church as a movement, in which the "new Catholic movements" are only one visible face of the new dimensions of being Church.[47]

This is where the vision of Vatican II becomes movement. Vision with no movement is destined to remain private; a movement with no vision is simply a physical phenomenon. The vision of Vatican II has changed the Church; the new feature of the Church as a movement is nothing less than an undeniable evidence of the many fruits of the council.

Dr. Massimo Faggioli *is Assistant Professor in the Department of Theology at the University of St. Thomas in St. Paul, MN.*

DISCUSSION QUESTIONS

1. Is there a relationship between "political views" and "theological interpretations of the council"?
2. What are the documents that need to be more studied by clergy and laity engaged in pastoral work?
3. What is next in the work of interpretation and reception of Vatican II?

SUGGESTED READINGS

Massimo Faggioli. *Vatican II: The Battle for Meaning*. Mahwah NJ/New York: Paulist Press, 2012.

Mark Massa. *The American Catholic Revolution: How the Sixties Changed the Church Forever.* New York: Oxford University Press, 2010.

John W. O'Malley. *What Happened at Vatican II?* Cambridge MA: Belknap Press of Harvard University Press, 2008.

David G. Schultenover, ed. *Vatican II: Did Anything Happen?* New York: Continuum, 2007.

NOTES

1. Paul VI, in *Acta Synodalia Sacrosancti Concilii Oecumenici Vaticani II*. Cura et studio Archivi Concilii Oecumenici Vaticani. (Città del Vaticano: Typis Polyglottis Vaticanis 1970-1999), vol. IV/7, p. 661. See also Peter Hünermann, "The Final Weeks of the Council," in *History of Vatican II*, vol. V, ed. Giuseppe Alberigo,

English version ed. Joseph A. Komonchak (Maryknoll, NY: Orbis, 2006), 474.

2. See Massimo Faggioli, *Vatican II: The Battle for Meaning* (Mahwah NJ/New York: Paulist Press, 2012).

3. See Bernard Häring, *Il concilio comincia adesso* (Alba, Italy, 1966).

4. See John W. O'Malley, *What Happened at Vatican II?* (Cambridge MA: Belknap Press of Harvard University Press, 2008) and *History of Vatican II*, vol. V, ed. Giuseppe Alberigo, English version ed. Joseph A. Komonchak (Maryknoll, NY: Orbis, 2006).

5. *"Quelle table! Il y a des piles de livres et de revues partout: sur la table, sur les chaises, par terre! Quel boulot!!!"*: Yves Congar, *Mon journal du concile*. Presented and annotated by Éric Mahieu (Paris: Cerf, 2002), vol. 2, p. 517.

6. See Étienne Fouilloux, "Essai sur le devenir du catholicisme en France et en Europe occidentale de Pie XII à Benoît XVI" *Revue théologique de Louvain* 42 (2011): 526-57.

7. See Denis Pelletier, *La crise catholique: religion, société, politique en France, 1965-1978* (Paris: Payot, 2002).

8. See Lisa Sowle Cahill, "Moral Theology after Vatican II," and Lisa Woodcock Tentler, "Souls and Bodies: The Birth Control Controversy and the Collapse of Confession," in *The Crisis of Authority in Catholic Modernity*, eds. Michael J. Lacey and Francis Oakley (New York: Oxford University Press, 2011), 193-224 and 293-315.

9. About this, see John T. Noonan, Jr., *A Church That Can and Cannot Change: The Development of Catholic Moral Teaching* (Notre Dame, Ind.: University of Notre Dame Press, 2005).

10. See *Vatican II: Assessment and Perspectives: Twenty-five Years After (1962-1987)*, ed. René Latourelle (New York: Paulist Press, 1988-89).

11. See Heribert Schmitz, "Tendenzen nachkonziliarer Gesetzgebung. Sichtung und Wertung," *Archiv fu?r katholisches Kirchenrecht* 146 (1977): 381-419.

12. See *Fundamental Theology. Doing Theology in New Places*, eds. Jean-Pierre Jossua and Johann Baptist Metz (New York, Seabury Press 1979: issue 115, 5/1978 of the journal *Concilium*); *Le*

Déplacement de la theologie, ed. J. Audinet et al. (Paris: Beauchesne, 1977).

13. See Daniele Menozzi, "Opposition to the Council," in *The Reception of Vatican II*, eds. Giuseppe Alberigo, Jean-Pierre Jossua, and Joseph A. Komonchak (Washington D.C.: The Catholic University of America Press, 1987), 325-48.

14. About the council of Trent as a paradigm, see Paolo Prodi, *Il paradigma tridentino. Un'epoca della storia della Chiesa* (Brescia: Morcelliana, 2010).

15. See Andrea Riccardi, *Il potere del papa da Pio XII a Giovanni Paolo II* (Roma-Bari: Laterza, revised edition, 1993).

16. See George Weigel, *The End and the Beginning. Pope John Paul II: The Victory of Freedom, the Last Years, the Legacy* (New York: Doubleday, 2010) to be compared now with the counter-narrative offered by Andrea Riccardi, *Giovanni Paolo II. La biografia* (Cinisello B.: San Paolo, 2011; translation in English forthcoming).

17. Cfr. Joseph P. Chinnici, "An Historian's Creed and the Emergence of Postconciliar Culture Wars," *The Catholic Historical Review* 94 (2008): 219-44; Joseph Chinnici, "Reception of Vatican II in the United States," *Theological Studies* 64/3 (2003): 461-94; see also T.J. Shelley, "Vatican II and American Politics," *America Magazine*, October 13, 2003.

18. Cfr. Giovanni Miccoli, *La Chiesa dell'anticoncilio. I tradizionalisti alla riconquista di Roma*, Roma-Bari 2011.

19. Cfr. Lieven Boeve, "'La vraie réception de Vatican II n'a pas encore commencé'. Joseph Ratzinger, Révelation et autorité de Vatican II", in *L'autorité et les autorités. L'herméneutique théologique de Vatican II*, eds. Gilles Routhier et Guy Jobin (Paris: Cerf, 2010), 13-50.

20. See Massimo Faggioli, "Il Vaticano II come 'costituzione' e la 'recezione politica' del concilio," *Rassegna di Teologia* 50 (2009): 107-22, and Massimo Faggioli, "Vatican II comes of age," *The Tablet*, 11 April 2009.

21. About this see Faggioli, *Vatican II: The Battle*, 24-35.

22. See Samuel P. Huntington, *The Third Wave: Democratization in the Late Twentieth Century* (Norman; London: University of Oklahoma Press, 1991).

23. See, for example, *Vatican II: Renewal within Tradition*, eds. by Matthew L. Lamb and Matthew Levering (New York: Oxford University Press, 2008).

24. See François Nault, "Comment parler des textes conciliaires sans les avoir lus?," in *L'autorité et les autorités. L'herméneutique théologique de Vatican II*, eds. Gilles Routhier et Guy Jobin (Paris: Cerf, 2010) 229-46.

25. See *Herders Theologischer Kommentar zum Zweiten Vatikanischen Konzil*, eds. Hans Jochen Hilberath and Peter Hünermann (Freiburg i.B.: Herder, 2004-2005).

26. About the development of the debate, see Massimo Faggioli "Concilio Vaticano II: bollettino bibliografico (2000-2002)," *Cristianesimo nella Storia*, 24/2 (2003): 335-60; "Concilio Vaticano II: bollettino bibliografico (2002-2005)," *Cristianesimo nella Storia*, 26/3 (2005): 743-67; "Council Vatican II: Bibliographical Overview 2005-2007," *Cristianesimo nella Storia*, 29/2 (2008): 567-610; "Council Vatican II: Bibliographical Overview 2007-2010," *Cristianesimo nella Storia*, 32/2 (2011): 755-91.

27. See Christoph Theobald, *La réception du concile Vatican II, Vol. I. Accéder à la source* (Paris: Cerf, 2009).

28. Theobald, *La réception du concile Vatican II*, vol. I, 476-82.

29. About this shift in theology between the nineteenth and the twentieth centuries see also Avery Dulles, *Models of Revelation* (New York: Doubleday, 1983), 36-67. See also *Ressourcement: A Movement for Renewal in Twentieth-Century Catholic Theology*, ed. Gabriel Flynn and Paul D. Murray (Oxford: Oxford University Press, 2012).

30. About this see Riccardo Burigana, *La Bibbia nel concilio. La redazione della constituzione "Dei Verbum" del Vaticano II* (Bologna: Il Mulino, 1998).

31. About this see Massimo Faggioli, *True Reform: Liturgy and Ecclesiology in "Sacrosanctum Concilium"* (Collegeville MN: Liturgical Press, 2012).

32. See Andrea Grillo, *La nascita della liturgia nel XX secolo. Saggio sul rapporto tra movimento liturgico e (post-) modernità* (Assisi: Cittadella, 2003).

33. For the fundamental idea of "unity" related to Vatican II see John XXIII, encyclical *Ad Petri Cathedram*, June 29, 1959, and

John XXIII, opening speech of Vatican II, *Gaudet Mater Ecclesia*, October 11, 1962.

34. See Giuseppe Alberigo, "Sinodo come liturgia?," *Cristianesimo nella storia*, XXVIII/1 (2007): 1-40.

35. See Werner Stegmaier, "Heimsuchung. Das Dialogische in der Philosophie des 20. Jahrhunderts," in *Dialog als Selbstvollzug der Kirche?*, ed. Gebhard Fürst (Freiburg i.B.: Herder, 1997), 9-29.

36. See Peter Smulders, "La Chiesa sacramento della salvezza," and Jan L. Witte, "La Chiesa 'sacramentum unitatis' del cosmo e del genere umano," in *La Chiesa del Vaticano II. Studi e commenti intorno alla Costituzione dommatica Lumen gentium*, ed. Guilherme Barauna (Firenze: Vallecchi, 1965): 363-86 and 491-521. For the use of "sacramentum" in the ecclesiological debate at Vatican II see Daniele Gianotti, *I Padri della Chiesa al concilio Vaticano II. La teologia patristica nella Lumen Gentium* (Bologna: EDB, 2010).

37. See Raymond Loonbeek and Jacques Mortiau, *Un pionnier, Dom Lambert Beauduin (1873-1960). Liturgie et unité des chrétiens* (Louvain-la-Neuve: Collège Erasme, 2001, 2 vols.) vol. 1, 907-909. See also Jacques Mortiau and Raymond Loonbeek, *Dom Lambert Beauduin visionnaire et précurseur (1873-1960). Un moine au coeur libre* (Paris: Cerf, 2005).

38. About this, see Peter Hünermann, "Kriterien für die Rezeption des II. Vatikanischen Konzils," *Theologische Quartalschrift* 191 (2/2011): 126-47.

39. See O'Malley, *What Happened at Vatican II?* 305-307.

40. Marie-Dominique Chenu, "Un concile prophetique," in *Le Monde*, 12 October 1982.

41. See O'Malley, *What Happened at Vatican II?* 311.

42. *Testament of the Holy Father John Paul II*, in http://www.vatican.va/gpII/documents/testamento-jp-ii_20050407_en.html.

43. See Giuseppe Alberigo, "Concili e rappresentanza," in *Repraesentatio. Mapping a Keyword for Churches and Governance*, eds. Massimo Faggioli and Alberto Melloni (Berlin: LIT, 2006) 99-124.

44. See *Synod and Synodality. Theology, History, Canon Law and Ecumenism in New Contact*, eds. Alberto Melloni and Silvia Scatena (Münster: LIT, 2005).

45. See Laurent Villemin, "L'herméneutique de Vatican II:

enjeux d'avenir," in *Vatican II et la theologie*, eds. Philippe Bordeyne et Laurent Villemin (Paris: Cerf, 2006) 247-62.

46. See Massimo Faggioli, "Council Vatican II between Documents and Spirit: The Case of the New Catholic Movements," in *After Vatican II: Trajectories and Hermeneutics*, eds. James Heft and John W. O'Malley (Grand Rapids MI: Eerdmans, 2012), 1-22.

47. See Massimo Faggioli, *Breve storia dei movimenti cattolici* (Roma: Carocci, 2008; Spanish translation *Historia y evolución de los movimientos católicos. De León XIII a Benedicto XVI*, Madrid: PPC Editorial, 2011).

To the Rulers

Reading the Classics to Renew Hope

R. Scott Appleby

In our reflections upon the closing addresses of the Second Vatican Council, we are instructed to look to the future, not dwell upon the past. This is an impossible task, of course, and not only for an historian but also for anyone who recognizes that there is no such thing as past or future, only the present moment; the rest is a foreign country. And of course even the present moment is imagined—not fully comprehended but only envisioned, through a construal of what we know or imagine we know *now*.

Accordingly, my only tools for imagining the future are to ask what path we are on, where the road since the Council has led us, and where it might be headed. In reading the closing speeches, not least "To the Rulers," one is struck by their spirit of confidence, their grandeur. Yes, it is true that in embracing the future, the Council Fathers drew on Christian *faith* and *hope* as much as on coldly calculated, empirically grounded political and cultural analysis of the world as it presented itself in 1965. Nonetheless the *unqualified* nature of the statements directed "To Rulers" astonishes us:

> We proclaim publicly: We do honor to your authority and your sovereignty, we respect your office, we recognize your just laws, we esteem those who make them and those who apply them. But we have a sacrosanct word to speak to you and it is this: Only God is great. God alone is the beginning and the end. God alone is the source of your authority and the foundation of your laws.

From the vantage of 2012, such assertions *do* seem to emerge from a foreign country.

The theologian David Tracy has defined a *classic* as a "transcending" event, text or person, an image, symbol or ritual that imposes itself upon an interpreter and cannot be ignored or "gotten around."[1] Such an event must be dealt with; it transforms our way of seeing the world. After Freud, for example, we can no longer pretend that the conscious mind is the fullness of our mental life. Like it or not, Freud was a classic, as was Hitler; so was Marx and certainly Jesus. The French Revolution was a classic in Tracy's sense. Certainly the Cross is a classic symbol.

Think of the "classics" that have transformed our sensibilities in the forty-seven years since, in the address to rulers, Cardinal Lienart uttered what now almost seems a naïve declaration: "God alone is the source of your authority and the foundation of your laws."

Let us take one such classic: Iran's Islamic Revolution, the icon of the wave of fundamentalisms that erupted within Christianity, Judaism and Islam in the 1970s, accompanied by religious nationalist movements and political parties in India, Israel, Egypt and elsewhere, each claiming God as the source of their authority and the foundation of their proposed laws. How did states and governments and religions themselves react to this unanticipated surge of politicized and militarized religion? The political scientist Scott Hibbard traces the pattern whereby "ostensibly secular state actors sought to coopt the ideas and activists associated with religious fundamentalisms."[2]

A small mountain of literature, much of it by social scientists, explores how politicians recruited religious actors in Sudan, Sri Lanka, Iran, Israel and elsewhere to do their "dirty work," including the violent persecution of religious and ethnic minorities.[3] "The invocation of illiberal renderings of religious tradition provided state actors with a cultural basis for their claims to rule and an effective means of mobilizing popular sentiment behind traditional patterns of social and political hierarchy," Hibbard writes. As a result, "secular norms were displaced by exclusive forms of religious politics."[4]

A related classic event, so totemic that we refer to it merely as 9/11, provided secularists, as well as many "Vatican II Catholics," with an object lesson regarding the assertion that "God alone is the source of your authority and the foundation of your laws." After the classic events of global fundamentalism and 9/11, most of us Vatican II Catholics would soak such a statement in heavy irony, and sprinkle it with a dose of theological humility. If God is the source of political authority and the foundation of temporal laws, we nonetheless must ask a more complicated question: who on earth has the authority to interpret politics, to determine which laws are divinely ordained and which fall short? "Theological humility," writes the theologian Ellen Ott Marshall, "is an antidote to the divine endorsement. In a posture of theological humility, one very carefully articulates religious reasoning that relates in some way to reasoning informed by other sources of knowledge. But this is very different from placing God's mantel over a particular political effort."[5]

The documents of Vatican II cannot be read as "placing God's mantel over a particular political effort," or as authorizing a politicized religious presence in the fundamentalist or religious nationalist mode. As *Gaudium et Spes* holds, "The Church, by reason of her role and competence, is not identified in any way with the political community nor bound to any political system." [76] Neither, however, does the Council allow for a complete separation between Catholicism and politics. "The Church and the political community in their own fields are autonomous and independent from each other. Yet both, under different titles, are devoted to the personal and social vocation of the same men. The more that both foster sounder cooperation between themselves with due consideration for the circumstances of time and place, the more effective will their service be exercised for the good of all." [76] Left ambiguous in such typical conciliar formulations are questions that have become ever more pressing in the intervening years: Is the Church the proper arbiter of secular legislation? Were the Council Fathers suggesting that the prophetic function of Christianity extends beyond moral critique to legislative oversight? "To the Rulers" does not go that far, but does leave the Church some wiggle room: "We proclaim publicly: We do honor to your authority and your sovereignty, we respect your office, we recognize your just laws, we esteem those who make them and those who apply them."

Laws that are unjust, the statement suggests, deserve no such recognition.

Alas, the Church's competence to discern between just and unjust laws has been called into question by a wide range of critics, including Catholics themselves, in the wake of the international sexual abuse crisis. The classic, according to Tracy, cannot be limited to a context. It has the power to "interpret the interpreter" and carries "an excess of meaning."[6] The sexual abuse crisis cannot be "gotten around"; the disgrace of priestly abuse of children and lack of public repentance of the hierarchy is a devastating sign of our times. It has shaped sensibilities ineradicably; indeed, in its consciousness-shaping impact, the crisis is the Vatican II of the current generation of young adult Catholics. Ironically, the Church confronts the fact that its credible accusers include many who rejected restrictive Catholic sexual norms and who were then roundly castigated by Church officials as libertines and hedonists. Yet these "dissenters" were able to recognize and enforce taboos around morally despicable behavior that many bishops permitted.

Religious freedom, then and now

The retreat from the Second Vatican Council's conditional affirmation of the humanist orientation of the secular world, including the sciences, and the Council Father's hope for collaboration between Church and world in defense of human dignity is nowhere more evident than in contemporary controversies regarding the status of same-sex unions, or the question of whether Catholic institutions in the United States must cover contraception, sterilizations and abortifacients as part of their staff's health insurance plans. The episcopal rhetoric is a world apart from that of Cardinals Lienart, Alfrink and Colombo back in December 1965. The historian wonders: What would the great Americanist of the late nineteenth century, John Lancaster Spalding, Bishop of Peoria, make of his early twenty-first-century successor, Daniel Jenky, CSC, who has compared the American president to Stalin and Hitler and who rails against Catholic politicians who "have their pictures taken with the hierarchy" and "have conspicuous crosses on their forehead with ashes" but who "not only do not live their faith, they collaborate in the assault against their faith"[7]? To Bishop Jenky the future is bleak, indeed, given "the intensity of hatred against Catholic Christianity in elements of our culture [which] is just astounding." And how would Joseph Cardinal Bernardin, the former Archbishop of Chicago and the prototype Jadot appointment, have responded, had he still been alive in 2010, when the Illinois legislature voted to legalize same-sex civil unions, a move which led to the closure of Catholic foster care services? We know how his successor reacted. Cardinal Francis George of Chicago, summing up apocalyptic rhetoric of the highest caliber, predicted: "I will die in bed, my successor will die in prison and his successor will die a martyr in the public square."[8]

How do we account for this sea change, and what does it portend for the future? First, we must recognize that the enshrinement of religious freedom as the cornerstone of Roman Catholic participation in the modern human rights movement was arguably the signal achievement of Vatican II. Interpreted as the right to preach and proclaim the Gospel, and to conduct its mission in all societies, religious freedom is also the hermeneutical principle for evaluating the proper relationship between Church, state and society. *Gaudium et Spes* sets this relationship forth as follows:

> The Church herself makes use of temporal things insofar as her own mission requires it. She, for her part, does not place her trust in the privileges offered by civil authority. She will even give up the exercise of certain rights which have been legitimately acquired, if it becomes clear that their use will cast doubt on the sincerity of her witness or that new ways of life demand new methods. It is only right, however, that at all times and in all places, the Church should have true freedom to preach the faith, to teach her social doctrine, to exercise her role freely among men, and also to pass moral judgment in those matters which regard public order when the fundamental rights of a person or the salvation of souls require it. In this, she should make use of all the means—but only those—which accord with the Gospel

and which correspond to the general good according to
the diversity of times and circumstances. [76]

Our guiding text, "To the Rulers," echoes and amplifies this principle:

> And what does this Church ask of you after close to
> 2,000 years of experiences of all kinds in her relations
> with you, the powers of the earth? What does the
> Church ask of you today? She tells you in one of the
> major documents of this council. She asks of you only
> liberty, the liberty to believe and to preach her faith, the
> freedom to love her God and serve Him, the freedom to
> live and to bring to men her message of life. Do not fear
> her. She is made after the image of her Master, whose
> mysterious action does not interfere with your preroga-
> tives but heals everything human of its fatal weakness,
> transfigures it and fills it with hope, truth and beauty.

How has the passage of time conditioned our understanding of this
cornerstone right and principle of religious freedom? In light of
this new understanding, how might the future unfold?

To take the first question first, we must acknowledge that during the half-century since Vatican II the concept of religious freedom
has become *culturally contested, politically charged, plural in meaning and
inextricably tied to the exceedingly fraught question of what counts as religion*. The historical roots, religious and philosophical warrants, legal
interpretations, theological and political meanings, and divergent
practices of religious freedom are matters of intense debate and often
fierce disagreement. At the very least, we now know to proceed with
appropriate methodological humility in making claims about "the
universality of religious freedom." Indeed, we have mounds of evidence on the *abrogation* of religious freedom. Roger Finke and Brian
Grimm's recent *tour d'horizon* of religious persecution around the
world is sobering. Finke and Grim argue that even small violations
of religious freedom (often in the form of seemingly innocuous regulations) can open the door to an erosion of other freedoms and
invite various forms of religious persecution.[9]

Among the more controversial issues, and not only among

Muslims, is the freedom to change religions, or to leave a religious community altogether. The argument concerning whether the pastoral orientation of Vatican II succeeded in renewing the Church or accelerated the exodus of younger generations, remains a touchstone for cultural warriors in the American church, but there is no doubt that "lapsed Catholics" number in the millions and that the number of younger Catholics leaving or never committing to the Church continues to rise. This dimension of "religious freedom"—freedom of exit, increasingly popular within pluralistic societies with open marketplaces of religion and spirituality—failed to temper the enthusiasm of the bishops fifty years ago, but it has become a matter of enduring concern for their successors.

And of course "religious freedom" is not free from manipulation by ideological and hegemonic forces. "Freedom *from* religion" has become a battle cry among some populations abroad, including religious communities, who interpret "religious freedom," and particularly the International Religious Freedom Act of the U.S. Congress, as a thinly veiled warrant for aggressive proselytism on the part of evangelical Christians supported by American power.[10] The fear in some quarters that one's own people can be converted by the "other," has become pronounced at a time of religious migration and upheaval. Such fear has generated support in some countries for laws and regulations restricting religion and religious freedom. More than 70 percent of the world's people live in societies in which there are severe government restrictions on religious practice. The greatest restrictions on religion are in place in the Middle East/North Africa and in South Asia. These restrictions contribute to tensions between religious groups in Afghanistan, Egypt, India, Iran, Iraq, Pakistan, and Yemen. The emergence and maturation of democratic Islamic politics, for example, has been retarded in these nations by the exclusion of some religiously-informed arguments, religious actors, and viable parties from the public sphere. Reporting and reflecting on this trend, a recent Task Force Report on religion in international affairs concluded:

> We must understand that in some cases, violence by religious actors is born of frustration with systemic discrimination against and repression of religious organizations

and movements that are the people's most trustworthy and responsible advocates for genuine social and economic progress and justice. In combating religious extremism, then, the United States must act with insight and discretion when advancing religious freedom, lest the responsible prosecution of terrorists dissolve into wholesale repression of religious actors, leading to the ironic and unintended consequence of deepening the problem of religiously inspired violence.[11]

The fear of American neo-imperialism reflects a suspicion of the modern nation-state that has become far more acute in our day than it was in the still cautiously optimistic sixties. The documents of Vatican II, while hardly giving the state a free pass, held out hope that democratically elected governments might join with the Church in building societies devoted to the common good. Other Catholic voices were less sanguine; among Thomas Merton's last words before his untimely death in 1968 was the admonition that believers could no longer depend on the good will of public institutions and officials.[12] In the intervening years, criticisms of the "hegemonic" and ruthlessly secular modern nation-state have mounted. Even a prominent supporter of the United Nations and the American-led international community recently described the western world order as a "liberal Leviathan."[13]

Classics of a different sort

What kind of future might unfold under such circumstances? Perhaps the answer is not as bleak as my observations to this point suggest. Indeed, there are some counterbalancing, benevolent "classics" of the past fifty years that offer signs of hope. I refer here to a person (John Paul II), a set of authoritative documents (*Evangelii Nuntiandi, Populorum Progressio, Caritas in Veritate*) and a movement (Catholic peacebuilding).

The Pope

The living witness and vibrancy accorded to religious freedom by the classic pontificate of John Paul II coincided with a shift in the privileged site of religious-political agency, from the state to civil society. The two developments were intertwined, in that John Paul's recognition and endorsement of religious pluralism, an implication of *Dignitatis Humanae*, reinforced and was reinforced by the pope's and the Church's turn to culture as the milieu for postconciliar Catholic activism. Civil society was the arena within which religion would henceforth strive to shape political culture.

The Church's affirmation of religious freedom as an article of religious as well as humanist faith, as the foundational principle of modern human rights, and as a necessary condition for the possibility of authentic human flourishing carried vast implications.[14] These implications were elaborated most visibly by Pope John Paul II, whose celebrated role inspiring Poland's Solidarity movement in its ultimately successful bid to overturn the Soviet-backed Communist regime was of a piece with his tireless pilgrimages to corners of the world where religious liberty was vulnerable to chauvinist, totalitarian or fundamentalist exclusions of minorities. A truly classic event unfolded before the eyes of the world; as the Harvard political scientist Samuel Huntington put it: who could possibly have predicted that the world's leading defender of religious freedom in the last quarter of the twentieth century would be…the Roman pontiff!

Today it is commonplace to find social scientists asserting that legal and constitutional protections for religious liberty, by enhancing religious pluralism and free speech, correlate positively with the building of a strong and vital civil society that is essential to the sustaining of democracy. A typical formulation runs as follows: "… religious communities are most likely to support democracy, peace and freedom for other faiths, and least likely to take up the gun or form dictatorships, when governments allow them freedom to worship, practice and express their faith freely and when religious communities in turn renounce their claims to permanent offices or positions of policy-making authority."[15] The growing salience of religion today, this line of thought continues, "is deepening the political significance of religious freedom as a universal human right and a source of social and political stability."[16]

These are bold and hopeful claims. Are they correct empirically and can they be stated without irony; that is, can religious freedom flourish without unintended consequences?

Given both the contested and culturally and religiously plural understandings of religious freedom *and* of religious obligations, the burden of proof falls upon those who generalize about the unambiguously positive consequences of religious freedom as a transnational or "universal" legal, cultural, religious, social regime. This burden of proof takes two forms. First, non-Western non-Christian nations must embed religious freedom in their own societies as an organic expression of the native cultural and social values of the nation or region in question. Second, suspicions that religious freedom is a cloak for aggressive proselytism in India, Saudi Arabia, Indonesia, Nigeria, etc. must be overcome by consistent evidence to the contrary. Any form of evangelization that operates under a robust regime of religious freedom must be based on *non-coercive* witness, with the definition of "coercion" understood in its broadest sense. Vatican II-era solidarity and witness through service sets the precedent. For example, *Evangelii Nuntiandi*, Paul VI's apostolic exhortation issued in 1975, on the tenth anniversary of the close of Vatican II, proclaims:

> 21. Above all the Gospel must be proclaimed by witness. Take a Christian or a handful of Christians who, in the midst of their own community, show their capacity for understanding and acceptance, their sharing of life and destiny with other people, their solidarity with the efforts of all for whatever is noble and good. Let us suppose that, in addition, they radiate in an altogether simple and unaffected way their faith in values that go beyond current values, and their hope in something that is not seen and that one would not dare to imagine. Through this wordless witness these Christians stir up irresistible questions in the hearts of those who see how they live: Why are they like this? Why do they live in this way? What or who is it that inspires them? Why are they in our midst? Such a witness is already a silent proclamation of the Good News and a very powerful and effective one. Here we have an initial act of evangelization. The above questions will ask, whether they are people to whom Christ has never been proclaimed, or

baptized people who do not practice, or people who live as nominal Christians but according to principles that are in no way Christian, or people who are seeking, and not without suffering, something or someone whom they sense but cannot name. Other questions will arise, deeper and more demanding ones, questions evoked by this witness which involves presence, sharing, solidarity, and which is an essential element, and generally the first one, in evangelization. [51][17]

What would it mean for all nations to protect the status of both majority *and minority* religious groups, including especially their ability to operate independently of the state; to have access to the public square on the basis of equality with each other and with nonreligious groups; and to be protected from coercion by the state or by other ethnic, nationalist, or religious groups? Catholics, it seems, are called to help resolve the tension between the need to foster the legitimate agency and autonomy of every religious community, whether a national minority or majority, that rejects terrorism and religious intolerance and the concern about the negative connotations the term "religious freedom" inspires among some religious communities, who see it as a code word for cultural fragmentation and erosion, often abetted by Western intervention.

Our "burden of proof" as Catholics, then, is to promote genuine religious freedom and its companion religious pluralism in ways that are viewed as promoting the common good and not as a form of religious chauvinism or neo-imperialism.

The Encyclicals

Pope Paul VI advanced the global agenda of the Council and set a path for the future by presiding over the final, crucial sessions that produced *Gaudium et Spes* and *Dignitatis Humanae* by internationalizing the Curia and college of cardinals, and by positioning the Church squarely in the moral and spiritual center of the emerging trinity of peace, justice and development that defines the renewed apostolate which, I am arguing in this paper, offers the Church's most compelling contemporary and future word to the rulers, to the temporal powers. Their primary responsibility is the stewardship of this world's societies; however, through a series of landmark encyclicals, Paul VI explicated and elaborated the commitments of the Church that follows from *Gaudium et Spes*'s famous opening lines identifying the joys and hopes, grief and anguish of this world with those of the Church. In his scene-setting encyclical on the new evangelization, the pope wrote:

> 30. ...Peoples, as we know, engaged with all their energy in the effort and struggle to overcome everything which condemns them to remain on the margin of life: famine, chronic disease, illiteracy, poverty, injustices in international relations and especially in commercial exchanges, situations of economic and cultural neo-colonialism sometimes as cruel as the old political colonialism. The Church, as the bishops repeated, has the duty to proclaim the liberation of millions of human beings, many of whom are her own children—the duty of assisting the birth of this liberation, of giving witness to it, of ensuring that it is complete. This is not foreign to evangelization...

> ...31. Between evangelization and human advancement—development and liberation—there are in fact profound links. These include links of an anthropological order, because the man who is to be evangelized is not an abstract being but is subject to social and economic questions. They also include links in the theological order, since one cannot dissociate the plan of creation from the plan of Redemption. The latter plan touches the very concrete situations of injustice to be combated and of justice to be restored. They include links of the eminently evangelical order, which is that of charity: how in fact can one proclaim the new commandment without promoting in justice and in peace the true, authentic advancement of man?[18]

In 1967 Pope Paul became the first pope to visit Africa, where he ordained bishops, encouraged the growth of an indigenous Church, and refined, reinforced and elaborated the themes of *Populorum*

Progressio, his groundbreaking encyclical, promulgated earlier that year, on human and economic development. The encyclical signaled the Vatican's intention to be the voice of "authentic human development" and the moral and spiritual guide to governmental, non-governmental and intergovernmental humanitarian relief and development organizations worldwide. Forty years later, Pope Benedict XVI revisited, updated and extended the themes of *Populorum Progressio* in his encyclical *Caritas in Veritate*.[19]

These various "mini-revolutions" in the realm of theology, ecclesiology and ethics led to the relocation of the Church's presence within the public sphere. And this expanded sense of mission also led to a shift that stands at the center of our discussion, namely, the evolution of Catholic missionary presence and support networks into an array of Catholic international non-governmental organizations (INGOs) and initiatives—I shall call these, collectively, a "movement"—that seek to incarnate Paul VI's famous dictum, "If you want peace, work for justice."

The movement

The collapse of the Soviet Union and the end of the Cold War—yet another classic event shaping the future of Vatican II—inaugurated a period when civil wars, ethnic and religious battles and regional conflicts have dominated the conflict arena. In this context, in which several states failed or were in the process of failing, and in which religious movements and ethnic groups challenged the state in providing social services—and, in some cases, became competing political authorities—religious leaders, not least Catholics, found themselves placed in a new and potentially powerful role as collaborators with, or alternatives to, governmental and other non-governmental actors. Catholic bishops, particularly in Africa and parts of Asia, find themselves called upon to perform a variety of public and civic functions, ranging from mediation between warring parties; to leadership of truth and reconciliation, human rights, or healing of memory commissions; to diplomacy or advocacy on behalf of the state itself.[20]

In this capacity the Roman Catholic Church is acting as a national as well as transnational agent in a new and distinctive way.

Top-down, Vatican-directed diplomacy is being complemented by local and national interventions in governance, policymaking, and public education. The most comprehensive approach to this attempted coordination and integration of local and global initiatives for peace is Catholic peacebuilding, the term of preference by a growing network of practitioners, scholars and church peace and justice workers.

Peacebuilders strive to comprehend the *longue durée* of a conflict—its full temporal, trans-generational range—and forge "solutions" commensurate to the deep historical rootedness of the inhumane personal, social and political relationships fueling the deadly violence. They see all the phases of these protracted conflicts—pre-violence, violence, and post-violence periods—as interrelated, such that violence prevention, early warning, conflict resolution, negotiated settlements, redress of grievances, human rights protection, retributive and restorative justice may occur in overlapping phases—and not only after the shooting has stopped and the latest round of peace talks are under way but also between and during recurrent episodes of deadly violence.

Accordingly, the various peacebuilding tools are deployed by people living in the local communities, those most directly victimized by the violence; by national elites in the government, business, education, religion and other sectors; and by diplomats, policymakers, scholars, international lawyers, religious leaders and other professionals operating at a geographical remove from the grassroots.[21]

Leading theorists of peacebuilding are keenly aware of how readily post–Cold War disputes over resources, borders, territory and governance can draw into the conflict the deepening and aggravating elements of ethnicity, religion, ideology and history. These dimensions of most contemporary hot conflicts lend them a certain resilience and spiritual-psychological depth that extends the cycles and rhythms of violence.

In this context, "Catholic internationalism" takes on a new dimension. Part of the appeal of the Church, whether in the form of a Catholic bishop or an INGO such as Catholic Relief Services, is precisely its transnational character. The commitment of local Catholic leaders to a multinational institution and chain of command with the moral authority of the Church carries at least three perceived advantages in countries struggling to overcome conflict or to experience sustainable economic growth. First, Catholic leaders may control, or be perceived to control, significant resources (personnel as well as financial) that flow from other centers, constituencies and religious orders. Second, the Catholic hierarchy enjoys the advantage of a local as well as global profile; that is, the Church tends to be trusted, owing to its rootedness in the people and historic (benevolent, charitable, etc.) presence in the local communities, while also possessing a certain political, social and even economic independence from local or national politics and politicians. Finally, the Catholic bishops are perceived to have influence with intergovernmental and international agencies, and with prominent states such as the United States, France, and the United Kingdom (the perception is often greater than the reality).

Catholic peace and justice advocates are present and active in societies where the Catholic Church is one among many actors engaging the state, operating within civil society, and/or influencing the realm of religion and culture. The Catholic presence and "clout," which varies widely from society to society and region to region, determines the resources and options available to the Church for peacebuilding activities and operations.

When Catholics think strategically about building peace, therefore, they do so with a heightened awareness of the importance of creating and sustaining alliances with other religious, ethnic and civic actors. While developing this and other strategies for maximizing the impact of the Catholic presence, however, they must not lose sight of the internal needs (and relative fragility) of the Catholic community itself.

Across the countries of sub-Saharan Africa the Church, while rarely a tiny minority, is by no means the exclusive or even dominant voice in the conversation about development, governance, equality, peace and conflict. Secular regimes and authoritarian rulers, tribal and ethnic leaders, and densely populated Muslim communities also constitute the patchwork quilt of society and political culture. In such settings, the ability of the Church to act as peacebuilder is governed by how strategically Catholics think and act in order to leverage their influence. How and where—in which sectors of society—this leveraging occurs varies from state to state, as the examples explored in this volume indicate. In countries suffering under failed or failing states, where governance is compromised by incompetence or corruption or both, the Church can quickly become the alternative to the state for people seeking basic services as well as national political leadership.

The Catholic worldview, of course, informs Catholicism's institutional presence at various levels of society, and shapes the Church's engagement with political leaders, civil society, religion and culture. By "the Catholic worldview," I mean the constellation of doctrines, symbols, rituals, ethical principles and instantiating practices that constitute an organic, unified vision of the world, of human nature and of God's plan for bringing both to their proper fulfillment, as anticipated in God's act of creation and revealed definitively in the Gospel of Jesus Christ.

There is ample evidence for affinities between the Catholic worldview and the sometimes unarticulated doctrines, rituals, symbols, ethical principles and instantiating practices that inform current peacebuilding practice, including religious as well as secular, and the work of humanitarian actors and relief and development workers, whatever their religious background. All prioritize the alleviation of human suffering and strive to provide nutrition, education, clean water, health care and equal access to employment. They would readily resonate with articles of Catholic social teaching such as the preferential option for the poor, solidarity, the priority of labor and stewardship of the environment.

The theologically-charged sacramental, communal and spiritual dimensions of the Catholic imagination, for example, are organically related, complementing and reinforcing one another to provide a transcendent, depth dimension to the Catholic understanding of human dignity and the ethical call to solidarity with the suffering and dispossessed. Belief in eternal life, the sanctifying and redeeming action of the Holy Spirit and the efficacy of Christ's promise to the Church threads through Catholic understandings and approaches to peacebuilding practices such as the accompaniment of victims, the reliance on ritual and prayer in healing and forgiveness, and "education for peace." Features of the Catholic imagination invariably play a role in judgments about what constitutes good governance, a just regime of human rights and the rule of law.

Is peacebuilding, as the concrete expression of the Church's mission of peace, justice and development, the wave of the future, the growing edge of the social tradition—or a tendency that will fade in the face of obstacles? As John Onaiyekan, the Roman Catholic archbishop of Abuja, Nigeria and president of the Episcopal Conference of Africa explained during an international conference of the Catholic Peacebuilding Network in Burundi in 2006: "We have no model or guide for this kind of ministry. Yes, we prefer to work through civil society. But I am the alternative to the state in Nigeria! And the government often needs an alternative!"[22]

It is also worth mentioning that Archbishop Onaiyekan is one of the most vigorous and enthusiastic proponents of Catholic peacebuilding, and that he has helped to bring several other African bishops on board.

Dr. R. Scott Appleby *is Professor of History and Regan Director of the Kroc Institute for International Peace Studies at the University of Notre Dame.*

DISCUSSION QUESTIONS

1. If religious freedom is the cornerstone of human rights, as the Church maintains, should the Church be held accountable for protecting human rights within the Church itself—for example, the right to free speech, the right to free assembly, the right to "a free press" (e.g., the right to publish one's ideas arguments regarding theological and ethical matters in dispute)?
2. If you had to prepare an address "To the Rulers" today and hoped to capture the bold and confident spirit of the Church looking ahead in 1965, what themes would you develop, what grounds for optimism would you emphasize?
3. Does the Church need a papal encyclical on peacebuilding as an apostolic calling for laity as well as religious and ordained? If not, why not? If so, what would be its major themes?

SUGGESTED READINGS

Kenneth L. Grasso and Robert P. Hunt, eds., *Catholicism and Religious Freedom: Contemporary Reflections on Vatican II's Declaration on Religious Liberty*. Lanham, MD: Sheed and Ward, 2006.

Gerrie ter Haar, ed., *Religion and Development: Ways of Transforming the World*. NY: Columbia University Press, 2011.

Paul Christopher Manuel, Lawrence C. Reardon and Clyde Wilcox, eds., *The Catholic Church and the Nation-State: Comparative Perspectives*. Washington, D.C.: Georgetown University Press, 2006.

Robert J. Schreiter, R. Scott Appleby and Gerard F. Powers, eds., *Peacebuilding: Catholic Theology, Ethics and Praxis*. Maryknoll, NY: Orbis, 2010.

NOTES

1. David Tracy, *The Analogical Imagination: Christian Theology and the Culture of Pluralism* (New York: Crossroad, 1981), 119.

2. Scott W. Hibbard, *Religious Politics and Secular States: Egypt, India and the United States* (Baltimore: The Johns Hopkins University Press, 2010), 4.

3. Seyyed Vali Reza Nasr, *Islamic Leviathan: Islam and the Making of State Power* (New York: Oxford University Press, 2001); Francis Deng, *War of Visions: Conflict Identities in Sudan* (Washington, DC: Brookings Institution Press, 1995).; David Little, *Sri Lanka: The Invention of Enmity* (Washington, DC: United States Institute of Peace, 1994); Mark Tessler, "The Origins of Popular Support for Islamist Movements," in *Islam, Democracy, and the State in North Africa*, ed. John Entelis (Bloomington: Indiana University Press, 1997).

4. Hibbard, *Religious Politics and Secular States*, xii.

5. Ellen Ott Marshall, "Religion, Peacebuilding and Global Governance," unpublished paper, 2012.

6. Tracy, *The Analogical Imagination*, 108, 296.

7. Bishop Daniel R. Jenky, CSC, "A Call to Catholic Men of Faith," April 14, 2012, *The Catholic Post*, http://www.thecatholicpost.com/post/PostArticle.aspx?ID=2440.

8. David Kerr, "Catholic politicians who attack Church should remember God's judgment," Rome, Italy, Feb 11, 2012 / 01:46 pm (CNA/EWTN News).

9. Brian J. Grim and Roger Finke, *The Price of Freedom Denied: Religious Persecution and Conflict in the 21st Century* (New York: Cambridge University Press, 2011).

10. The 1998 International Religious Freedom Act (IRFA) established at the Department of State an ambassador-at-large for international religious freedom to advance religious freedom using the tools of U.S. foreign policy. It also created a separate U.S. Commission on International Religious Freedom to act as a watchdog agency and provide independent policy recommendations.

11. R. Scott Appleby and Richard Cizik, *Engaging Religious Communities Abroad: A New Imperative for U.S. Foreign Policy* (Chicago: Chicago Council on Global Affairs, 2011).

12. "Merton: A Film Biography" (First Run Features, 1984).

13. G. John Ikenberry, *Liberal Leviathan: The Origins, Crisis and Transformation of the American World Order* (Princeton: Princeton University Press, 2011).

14. Endorsed by a vote of 2,308 to 70, *Dignitiatis Humanae* (The Declaration on Religious Liberty, promulgated by Pope Paul VI on December 7, 1965) includes this famous passage:

> 2. This Vatican Council declares that the human person has a right to religious freedom. This freedom means that all men are to be immune from coercion on the part of individuals or of social groups and of any human power, in such wise that no one is to be forced to act in a manner contrary to his own beliefs, whether privately or publicly, whether alone or in association with others, within due limits
>
> The council further declares that the right to religious freedom has its foundation in the very dignity of the human person as this dignity is known through the revealed word of God and by reason itself. This right of the human person to religious freedom is to be recognized in the constitutional law whereby society is governed and thus it is to become a civil right.

15. Monica Duffy Toft, Daniel Philpott, and Timothy Samuel Shah, *God's Century: Resurgent Religion and Global Politics* (New York and London: W.W. Norton & Company), 18.

16. Appleby and Cizik, *Engaging Religious Communities Abroad*, 41.

17. Pope Paul VI, *Evangelii Nuntiandi* [On Evangelization in the Modern World] (Washington, DC: Publications Office, United States Catholic Conference, 1976).

18. Ibid.

19. Pope Paul VI, "*Populorum Progressio* [On the Development of Peoples]" in Gremillion, ed., *The Gospel of Peace and Justice*, 390, http://www.vatican.va/holy_father/benedict_xvi/encyclicals/documents/hf_ben-xvi_enc_20090629.

20. For background, see R. Scott Appleby, "Catholic Peacebuilding," *America* (8 September 2003): 12–15.

21. R. Scott Appleby, "Peacebuilding and Catholicism: Affinities and Convergences," in Robert Schreiter, R. Scott Appleby and Gerard Powers, eds., *Peacebuilding: Catholic Theology, Ethics and Praxis* (New York: Orbis, 2011), 3-22.

22. Transcript of the Catholic Peacebuilding Network Conference, Bujumbura, Burundi, 2006.

To Women

If It Wasn't for the Women: Roman Catholic Women and Their Church

Diana L. Hayes

There is a saying in the black community: "If it wasn't for the women, where would we be?" The correct answer, obviously, is: "Nowhere!" Women make up over half of the population not just in the United States but throughout the world. Thus, if women are disengaged, uninvolved, made invisible or marginalized, we are in deep trouble. This African American proverb is very appropriate for the task that was set before me, namely to look at Pope Paul VI's statement "On Women" issued at the closing of the Second Vatican Council. My task, as I see it, is not to simply restate what was said then in that very brief statement, but to develop the themes to be found within it and connect them to the universal call for holiness for all of the baptized in the twenty-first century.

In the waning days of the Second Vatican Council in 1965, Pope Paul VI issued seven brief addresses on various topics. His address to women was one of these, only a page long but conveying the new openness and understanding that fit in with the more open and egalitarian tone set by the longer and more prominent documents such as *Lumen Gentium* and *Gaudium et Spes*. It affirmed, for many, their sense that the Church was actually coming to a fuller awareness of itself and its situation, its roles and responsibilities, within the global world that was slowly emerging. The Council, as we know, opened the doors to greater engagement and participation of women and their involvement in pastoral and political activities of the Church itself, expanding the ministries in which they could engage and the roles they could perform including those of theologians, teachers and proclaimers of the faith. In other words, women were called to participate alongside men in the three-fold priesthood of all of the faithful, as preachers, prophets, and queens (as opposed to kings!). This recognition was a small first step that has culminated in a journey of many miles by women of the Catholic Church who have sought to answer God's call to holiness. It is a path strewn with many obstacles and setbacks but also smoothed and fashioned by the willing hands of so many, male and female, who see in women's response to God's call hope for the ongoing viability of our Mother Church.

Almost fifty years have passed since that December day in 1965 when those seven short speeches were given. In a way, the document itself is somewhat anticlimactic after three years of powerful and definitive statements emerging from the deliberations of the Council Fathers, many of which touched on or included the roles, responsibilities, and rights of women in the Church and modern society.

Pope Paul VI addressed women of all states: girls, wives, mothers, and widows as well as consecrated virgins and women living alone. Calling attention to the Church's history of "having glorified and liberated woman," he also affirmed that the Church had "brought into relief her basic equality with man." But, as the Council had affirmed, the times were changing. What had been done in the past was insufficient in terms of what needed to be done for and on behalf of women in the world today, especially in light of the still persistent resistance to and at times antagonism towards women. He noted:

> …the hour is coming, in fact has come, when the vocation of woman is being achieved in its fullness, the hour in which woman acquires in the world an influence, an effect and a power never hitherto achieved. That is why, at this moment when the human race is undergoing so deep a transformation, women impregnated with the spirit of the Gospel can do so much to aid mankind in not failing.[1]

The Holy Father calls upon women as the protectors of the home and the first educators to pass on the traditions of their church and society while helping to prepare their children for an unforeseeable future, something women, as bearers of culture, have done throughout time. He also calls upon women living alone (what I assume we would call single women today) and consecrated virgins (presumably the religious) to work within society by being "guardians of purity, unselfishness, and piety" and addresses "women in trial", meaning, I assume, those women who are oppressed in various ways and struggling to survive, asking them to "retain courage" and "maintain patience." He concludes by naming as the task of women "to bring the spirit of [Vatican II] into institutions, schools, homes, and daily life. Women of the entire universe, whether Christian or non-believing, you to whom life is entrusted at this grave moment in history, it is for you to save the peace of the world."[2]

As I said, it is a very short document but a very challenging one as well. It upholds women's usual roles in the domestic sphere but also calls them outside those roles to be active and responsible participants in a changing world, one that needed the strength, courage, and perseverance of women in order to move forward into the future. Ivy Helman, in her work *Women and the Vatican*, summarizes this call: "This very short document beseeches women to use their special abilities of caring, truth, love, and guidance to help men become more life affirming. In this way women are charged with saving civilization from self-implosion and re-directing humanity to more loving, caring, and responsible ways to live on Planet Earth."[3]

This is certainly a daunting task which still seems to focus on what some would see as stereotypes of women as nurturers, etc. It is also interesting, in that the Holy Father's focus seems to be in making men more "human" or "life-affirming," a task which has engaged women, I believe, since Eve first encountered Adam. It is a heavy responsibility, indeed, saving the world, yet we are also urged to be "patient" as we seek change in society and, I assume, the Church as well.

The call to "maintain patience" is not new but a familiar admonition to those who have historically been marginalized and silenced. In order to bring the spirit of Vatican II to full and enriching life, women came to realize that they must at times lose patience with the snail-like progress too often encouraged. For, as Martin Luther King stated with regard to a similar admonition of patience to African Americans during this same time period:

> We know through painful experience that freedom is never voluntarily given by the oppressor; it must be demanded by the oppressed....For years now I have heard the word "Wait!" It rings in the ears of every Negro with piercing familiarity. This "Wait" has almost always meant "Never...." We must come to see...that "justice too long delayed is justice denied."[4]

But Vatican II was a beginning, indeed a major step forward in the Church's efforts to recognize and remedy wrongs that had persisted for so long a time, too often with its tacit approval. Change comes when least expected, however, and women were ready to receive the message of the Council and act upon it.

In the forty-five plus years since the end of the Second Vatican Council, what can we say about this document's themes and the present reality of women? The Holy Father was certainly correct when he, as in *Gaudium et Spes*, affirmed the "signs of the times" with regard to the opening of society and the Church to the greater engagement and participation of women. Since 1965, encouraged not only by the spirit of Vatican II but also, certainly in the United States, by that of the civil rights movement and the many liberation movements it spawned including that of women, we have witnessed the entrance of women into almost every level of society and to greater roles and responsibilities within the Church itself. Building upon the fundamental equality of all men and women as pronounced by God in the Genesis stories of creation (Gen 1:26-27, 2:5-7), we recognize and affirm that in Christ Jesus there is no superior or inferior in terms of gender, race, ethnicity or class (Gal 3:28). This opening of the Church to the world encouraged a multitude of women to embark upon vocations that emerged from the universal call to holiness of all of God's people.

The *Catechism of the Catholic Church*, taking as its source *Lumen Gentium: The Dogmatic Constitution on the Church*, states: "'All Christians in any state or walk of life are called to the fullness of Christian life and to the perfection of charity.' All are called to holiness: 'Be perfect, as your heavenly Father is perfect.'" (Matt 5:48)[5]

> In order to reach this perfection the faithful should use the strength dealt out to them by Christ's gift, so that… doing the will of the Father in everything, they may wholeheartedly devote themselves to the glory of God and to the service of their neighbor. Thus the holiness of the People of God will grow in fruitful abundance, as is clearly shown in the history of the Church through the lives of so many saints.[6]

We are all called to intimate union with God, a mystical union because "it participates in the mystery of Christ through the sacraments—the holy mysteries—and, in him, in the mystery of the Holy Trinity."[7] This understanding of a universal call to holiness in terms of the laity was relatively new and was spelled out in the Vatican II Decree on the Apostolate of the Laity as well as in *Lumen Gentium* and *Gaudium et Spes*: the Pastoral Constitution on the Church in the World. What changed is that the Church, redefined as the People of God that includes all Catholic Christians from laity through religious and priests, bishops and cardinals, to the Holy Father himself, are seen as equal in dignity and in their call to holiness. This equality is grounded in the understanding that, as human beings, we have been created in the image and likeness of God and thus have an innate dignity bestowed upon us through our creation that demands equality in the sight of God and all of humanity. As the Council Fathers affirmed in *Gaudium et Spes*:

> All men are endowed with a rational soul and are created in God's image; they have the same nature and origin and, being redeemed by Christ, they enjoy the same divine calling and destiny; there is here a basic equality between all men and it must be given ever greater recognition.
>
> … [F]orms of social or cultural discrimination in basic personal rights on the grounds of sex, race, color, social conditions, language or religion, must be curbed and

eradicated as incompatible with God's design. It is regrettable that these basic personal rights are not yet being respected everywhere, as is the case with women who are denied the chance freely to choose a husband, or a state of life, or to have access to the same educational and cultural beliefs as are available to men.[8]

Dennis Doyle, in his book *The Church Emerging From Vatican II*, states this understanding well:

> [*Lumen Gentium*] is emphasizing that in a most fundamental spiritual sense the members of the church are equal. By virtue of one's baptism, one is a full member of the church with a full share in God's grace insofar as one perseveres in love. When it comes to faith, spiritual dignity, grace, salvation, hope, and love, each member is invited to share fully. There are no second-class Catholics. There is no hierarchy when it comes to being called to holiness....Every member of the church is called to a life of holiness.[9]

As can be imagined, this was good news to many, but especially to women and Catholics of color who had often felt that they were second-class Catholics because of the ways they were treated by other Catholics: male and/or white.

This paved the way for a new or renewed understanding of the Church as the People of God on a pilgrim journey towards God and opened the doors for significant changes in how the Church saw itself, how it interacted with other churches and peoples, and, importantly, how it related to women who made up then and continue to make up today the great majority of the church. Women were challenged to rethink themselves and their relationship to the Church, and empowered to see themselves as equal members of the Church with perspectives that would enable the Church to be a fuller reflection of Jesus Christ.

Historically, as noted earlier, the Church has congratulated itself on its efforts to promote and celebrate women, yet many women had a very different perspective, seeing the church as more of an oppressive reality that limited them to the roles of mother, wife or consecrated virgin without the freedom to seek other paths. In reality, the Church was acting in keeping with society, which throughout the world was patriarchal and hierarchical, thereby strictly delineating the differences between males and females and construing the latter as the weaker sex needing protection and therefore limitations. These beliefs, which culminated in the egregious sin of sexism, among others, were rooted in an interpretation of Scripture and theology that was faulty because of its overriding belief that women were inferior beings requiring regulation.

After more than one and a half millennia, the Roman Catholic Church was finally beginning to recognize not only its own faults but also how those faults had impacted the world as a whole. This recognition of and opening to aspects of modernity was truly a breath of fresh air for the entire Church. Even though the Church still presented women's roles as mainly domestic, it also recognized their right to a job with a living wage and of their own choosing.

Although I was not born a Roman Catholic, but entered the Church at the age of thirty-two, I was very familiar with these restrictions and perspectives on women. When I was born in 1947, opportunities in life for women and persons of color were few and limited. As a person of African ancestry, I was hemmed in by racial stereotypes and discrimination, and limited in my choice of employment, educational opportunities, and participation in the political life of my country. At the same, there were additional restrictions placed upon me because of my gender. As a woman, I was again limited politically, socially, and religiously. My choice of careers was restricted to those considered suitable for a woman: nurse, secretary, teacher; my choice and even right to higher education was still a topic of discussion for others to pronounce upon, and my roles in the church of my birth (the A.M.E. Zion church) were limited to "appropriate" women's roles, such as members of auxiliary clubs attached to those of men or as secretaries and Sunday School teachers, etc., I was hemmed in on every side.

Today, that world has pretty much disappeared and cannot return despite the fervent wishes of some that it would. Just as you cannot step into the same river twice, you cannot return to a golden past, especially since for many it was not that golden. Truly, this change was the work of the Holy Spirit wending her way across the earth breathing the breath of God into places long cloaked in the darkness of oppressive and life-denying ideologies and forces.

But even today, I have never had the freedom to simply be a woman. I have always been a black woman, or more specifically, a working-class black woman. This has its benefits but also its problems as I and my sisters have struggled with our sisters of other racial and ethnic groups for recognition of the concerns of women of color while at the same time struggling with our black brothers for the right to "speak the truth, God's truth" to them and whomever we encounter. As a black woman, I cannot separate my racial/ethnic self from my gendered self; both have affected and continue to affect my life of faith and my choices in life. This is true for many women of color today. Yet the Church still persists in seeing these issues, including class, as separate and unequal in importance.

As a womanist theologian, that is a black female theologian who sides with and fights for the liberation of all who are oppressed regardless of race, class, gender or sexuality, I find it challenging to be a Roman Catholic today. This Church was not a part of my early life of faith yet when I was called into it as I believe I was, I found a great deal to affirm my faith in a just and loving God. At the same time, as I began and continued my theological studies I found much that challenged and discouraged me.

I was told often that I was a feminist, a naming I never accepted, not because of the Church's concerns regarding the movement but because of the lack of relevancy to my own experience that I found in it. As I stated earlier, as a black woman I was confronted on a daily basis with issues of not just gender or sexuality but race and class. Thus, my concern was and continues to be a focus on the liberation of women: all women, yes, but in ways that also liberate them from the ideologies of not just sexism but also racism and classism. These are intertwined and multiplicative; they cannot be addressed singularly but only in a holistic way that reveals the human construction of these ideologies and the contributions that the Christian churches have made to these constructions.

This is a challenging time to be a woman, both in the United States and the Roman Catholic Church. What many, male and female alike, see as a rabid backlash against the immense gains made in human and civil rights in the last forty-plus years is spewing forth in a volcanic unleashing of legislative shifts and efforts that diminish rather than enhance the dignity of all human beings and reflect a misogyny still deeply embedded in far too many. It requires the inspired commitment of all of us to overcome these biases.

The vision of Vatican II was one of *aggiornamento*, the opening of the doors and windows of the Church to the wider world. Many feel this was absolutely necessary while others were and apparently still are appalled. Today, many want to move that vision forward while others seem to want to put it in reverse. I do not think this is the time or place to discuss some of the more hot-button issues of today that affect not just women but all of society such as that of abortion, birth control and contraceptives, and women's ordination. But it must be recognized that these are issues that will not simply fade away as women continue to struggle for basic human rights as persons created in the image and likeness of God. They are the only ones who can truly speak from their experience as women from every walk of life and they must be allowed and encouraged to do so. But let me follow my mandate and discuss how far we have come while acknowledging that we are not yet the church that the vast majority of women and men want and are still journeying towards.

For me, and many women, the Church has been and continues to be a source of liberation. I entered the church in 1979 as an adult who had practiced law for several years. I was called by God, I believe, for a task that at the time was not very clear and even today seems at times a bit foggy. But I was inspired by John Paul II and what I saw and still see as his openness and willingness to engage in the world, especially his perspective on social justice which to me, as a womanist liberation theologian, were grounded in not just the Church's social teachings but also the best of insights from leading Latin American liberation theologians. I only wished that more attention would be paid to the equally challenging liberation theologies of the United States, especially black and Hispanic. But perhaps, on reflection, after the Vatican response to Feminist and Latin American Theologies, it is sometimes better not to be noticed.

In the period between 1965 and today, we have seen many changes within the Church with regard to women, most of them very good. I know that I myself would not be standing here before you today as a Catholic theologian if it had not been for the Council with its affirmation of women's call to holiness and responsibility to learn of her faith and pass that knowledge on to others. As I stated earlier, the affirmation that women should and did participate fully in the threefold priesthood of preacher, prophet, and queen empowered women to seek greater opportunities within the Church as well as the world at large. When I entered theological studies, I did not realize that I was a first, the first African American woman to enter the pontifical degree program and eventually the first to receive the pontifical doctorate. I did not know at the time that I was breaking new ground along with many other women. Being a first, I came to realize, can be very difficult since you have to break down barriers, conscious and unconscious, erected by others to "keep you in your place" for as long as they can.

Fortunately, I am a very stubborn person and, like many women today, refused to take no as a final answer. I and others recognized that our "coming to voice" and sharing of our experiences benefited the Church as a whole. We sought and continue to seek to speak the truth of our lives recognizing that we have been graced by God to teach, preach, and prophesy. I was not alone on my theological journey as I encountered women, Protestant and Catholic, who were walking boldly through doors hesitantly creaking open. By our actions, we affirmed that we were divinely created and called to a holiness that required study and preparation but would over time enable us to participate more fully at every level of our churches and our society.

One of the most significant changes took place in religious life as, called to deepen their spirituality and rethink their mission based on their Order's history and the needs of the modern Church and humanity, many women's religious Orders began to enter more fully into the world to truly serve as leaven. Sisters abandoned or modified their habits, pondered and eventually rewrote their constitutions and emerged into the world re-born. Although many maintained their roles as teachers at every level from elementary school to college, others, seeking to be of greater value to their Church and congregation, entered into higher education, spending summer after summer on hot campuses like Catholic University of America studying theology, church history and canon law. The women's religious orders have today become the best models for the collegiality and subsidiarity called for in Vatican II. They are truly the Church in microcosm bringing the light of faith to all parts of the world.

I was stunned when I was told that historically when religious women were allowed to come to summer classes at CUA, they had to sit outside in the hall! I could not believe it. But these and many other restrictions soon fell, to the consternation of some and the joy of others. Studying at the graduate level enabled us to model the "new" Catholic woman, one who sought to contribute to and participate in the works of the Church in every way open to her.

Since the end of Vatican II in 1965, there have been a number of documents on women in the Church issued by Bishops, the United States Conference of Catholic Bishops, and the Vatican. Although many of these statements are on the issue of the ordination of women, they and others also follow through, albeit to a limited extent, on the promise of Vatican II and Paul VI's address to women developing what Helman calls a "theology of womanhood" rooted in women's roles and responsibilities as creators and nurturers of new life. Pope John Paul II, in particular, building upon Vatican II, has affirmed the universal call to holiness of all the faithful and taken steps to eradicate vestiges of the older "anti-woman" and patriarchal stance or tone of the Church, including reinstating Mary Magdalene as the Apostle to the Apostles as she was the first to see the risen Christ and to be commissioned by him, elevating St. Therese of Lisieux to Doctor of the Church, and other steps, especially with regard to Mary, the Mother of God. He urged women to participate in the life of the Church at every level and appointed women for the first time to many Vatican committees and institutions. In his apostolic letter *Mulieris Dignitatem*, the Holy Father speaks in terms of complementarity noting that "both man and woman are human beings to an equal degree"[10] and are called to collaborate with each other in the work of the Kingdom. He states:

> ...men and women, created as a "unity of the two" in their common humanity, are called to live in a communion of love, and in this way to mirror in the world the

communion of love that is in God, through which the
Three Persons love each other in the intimate mystery of
the one divine life.[11]

Some see this understanding as a limitation on the role of
women, and in the sense that it is used to counter arguments for the
admission of women to all offices in the Church, this is true. But
arguably it can also simply be seen as a recognition of the differences that do exist between men and women that are not limited to
the biological. As a womanist, the idea of complementarity is one
that bears fruit in the black community in our relationships with
black men who are our fathers, uncles, brothers, nephews, and
sons. As black women, we realize that the black community would
not have survived without the collaboration of both men and
women working towards freedom first from slavery and then from
second class citizenship and other forms of discrimination.
Although many would be correct in saying that the Protestant black
Church still suffers greatly from misogyny and sexism as do, sadly,
many Christian churches, it also must be acknowledged that they
have come a long way as now women are ordained alongside men
and even appointed or elected as Bishops. We are in trouble in the
black community today because that shared solidarity, that sense of
collaboration that brought us so far, has begun to fray as we, like
too many today, succumb to the seductions of an increasingly mate-
rialistic, individualistic, and consumerist society. But the model is
still there and working in many areas and communities.

In the Catholic Church, great progress has indeed been made.
Although I am not sure that I would agree with Mary Ann
Glendon's designation of Pope John Paul's writings as evidence of
a "new feminism," one that he calls for to replace what has been
designated as "radical feminism," I also do not believe that he was
as anti-woman as others have claimed. Misogyny, and its accompa-
nying hatreds and prejudices, is, indeed, still alive and well in our
Church, a sin that holds us back and leads us astray as we travel on
our pilgrim journey towards God. But I believe it cannot last in the
face of the countless numbers of women who, especially in light of
the persistent decline in priestly vocations, have stepped in and
offered their services to their Church. There are more women

studying theology today than ever before, and despite claims to the contrary, the majority are getting their degrees from Catholic institutions and are fully sound in their doctrine. Again, if it wasn't for the women, where would we as Church truly be?

Women are the face of the future Church, a face increasingly of color, which is now coming into being despite efforts to drag us into a past that in actuality never existed. As the American bishops have affirmed "...the true face of the Church appears only when and if we recognize the equal dignity of women and men and consistently act on that recognition."[12] John Paul II, in *Ordinatio Sacerdotalis*, makes a similar point: "[the role of women] is of capital importance...for the rediscovery by believers of the true face of the Church."[13] He calls upon female saints and martyrs of old and women of today who have offered and continue to offer their gifts to the Church in numerous ways. These gifts differ within the ranks of women as well as between women and men, but all are gifts from a loving God who has called them into being and commissioned them to serve his body, the Church. As the American Bishops acknowledged, "The Church better fulfills its mission when the gifts of all its members are engaged as fully as possible. Women are essential in ministry both within the Church and to the world. The diversity of women's gifts and talents should be celebrated."[14]

Paul VI's call for us to recognize the signs of the times and bring forth the gifts of women for the betterment of our beloved Church still rings true today. Women, in ever growing numbers, single and vowed, married and widowed, have responded to God's call and continue to do so.

I am reminded of the words of Sojourner Truth, a former slave, who spoke at a Women's Convention in Akron, OH, in 1851. Speaking to an audience of men and women, all white, who clearly did not want her to speak, she expounded on the question of who is and is not a woman and what their goals should be. She concluded by stating the following, speaking regarding Eve, the mother of us all: "If the first woman God ever made was strong enough to turn the world upside down all alone, these women together ought to be able to turn it back, and get it right side up again. And now they are asking to do it, the men better let them."[15]

The door has been opened too wide to ever be closed again.

We cannot go back because the past is just that, it is gone, over with. Too much has changed within Church and society. Nostalgia is fine in its place but our emphasis should be on preparing for the future, one coming into being as we speak. Much has been accomplished but much more still needs to be done for the fullness of the vision of Vatican II to be realized. Women of faith, in company with, not apart from, men of faith, must work together to bring into full uncontested being the reality of the human dignity of all human beings and their universal call to holiness, a call that impels them to work for the betterment of their Church and their world. The Church has given women the responsibility of "bettering" the world and especially the men who inhabit it. That mandate applies to the Church itself as well as it is a part of the global world. It is long past time that we be allowed to do the work we are capable of doing for the betterment of all in response to God's call.

Dr. Diana L. Hayes *is Professor Emerita of Systematic Theology in the Department of Theology at Georgetown University.*

DISCUSSION QUESTIONS

1. What does it mean to be a Catholic woman today?
2. What do women contribute to the life and work of the Church?
3. What do you see as your role(s) as a woman in the Church today and has this changed in any way during your life; how and why?
4. How do women, individually and as a whole, participate in the universal call to holiness?
5. Do you understand the Church's teaching on complementarity? Do you see it as empowering or restricting women?

SUGGESTED READINGS

Dennis Doyle. *The Church Emerging From Vatican II*. New London, CT: Twenty-Third Publications, 2009.

Ivy Helman. *Women and the Vatican: An Exploration of Official Documents*. Maryknoll, NY: Orbis Books, 2012.

Carmel McEnroy. *Guests in Their Own House: The Women of Vatican II*. New York: The Crossroad Publishing Company, 1996.

NOTES

1. Address of Pope Paul VI to Women (8 December 1965), http://www.vatican.va/holy_father/paul_vi/speeches/1965/docu ments/hf_p-vi_spe_19651208_epilogo-concilio-donne_en.html, paragraph 1.

2. Paul VI, Address to Women, paragraphs 5 and 6.

3. Ivy Helman. *Women and the Vatican: An Exploration of Official Documents* (Maryknoll, NY: Orbis Books, 2012), 11.

4. "Letter from a Birmingham Jail" in James M. Washington, ed., *A Testament of Hope: The Essential Writings and Speeches of Martin Luther King, Jr.* (San Francisco: Harper One, 1990), 292.

5. *Catechism of the Catholic Church* (New York: Doubleday, 1995) 542, paragraph 2013.

6. *Catechism of the Catholic Church.*

7. *Catechism of the Catholic Church*, paragraph 2014.

8. *Gaudium et Spes: The Church in the Modern World* in Austin Flannery, OP, ed., *Vatican Council II: The Conciliar and Post Conciliar Documents*, vol. 1 (Northport, NY: Costello Publishing Company, 2005), 929, paragraph 29.

9. Dennis Doyle. *The Church Emerging From Vatican II* (New London, CT: Twenty-Third Publications, 2009), 116.

10. *Mulieris Dignitatem* www.vatican.va/holy_father/john_paul_ii/apost_letters'documents/hf_jp-ii_apl_1508, March 13, 2012, paragraph 6.

11. Pope John Paul II, *Mulieris Dignitatem*, paragraph 7.

12. USCCB, "Strengthening the Bonds of Peace" A Pastoral Reflection on Women in the Church and in Society" (1994), www.old.usccb.org/laity/bonds.html, March 12, 2012, 3.

13. Pope John Paul II, *Ordinatio Sacerdotalis* (Washington, DC: USCC Publishing Services, 1994), 3.

14. USCCB, "Strengthening the Bonds of Peace," 3.

15. Sojourner Truth, Speech at Akron, OH, Women's Convention (1851), www.fordham.edu/halsall/mod/sojtruth-woman.asp.

To the Poor, the Sick, and the Suffering

Roberto S. Goizueta

On September 11, 1962, on the eve of the Second Vatican Council, Pope John XXIII taped a radio message addressed to "all the Christian faithful" and broadcast around the world. In that address, the Holy Father set the tone for the council by declaring that: "Confronted with the underdeveloped countries, the church presents itself as it is and wishes to be, the church of all, and particularly the Church of the Poor."[1] At the council's adjournment three years later, Pope Paul VI joined the Council Fathers in addressing a message to all "the poor, the sick, and suffering" of the world:

> All of you who feel heavily the weight of the cross, you who are poor and abandoned, you who weep, you who are persecuted for justice, you who are ignored, you the unknown victims of suffering, take courage. You are the preferred children of the kingdom of God, the kingdom of hope, happiness and life. You are the brothers of the suffering Christ, and with Him, if you wish, you are saving the world. This is the Christian science of suffering, the only one which gives peace. Know that you are not alone, separated, abandoned or useless. You have been called by Christ and are His living and transparent image. In His name, the council salutes you lovingly, thanks you, assures you of the friendship and assistance of the Church, and blesses you.[2]

At the very heart of the Second Vatican Council's deliberations, which notably included episcopal voices from throughout the

Third World, was the Church's attempt to retrieve the Gospel as "Good News for the Poor" in the contemporary context of a world church. Yet "the poor, the sick, and suffering" addressed here are no mere objects of Christian charity or even Christian justice; they are Christ's "living and transparent image." The good news proclaimed to them is: "You are the preferred children of the kingdom of God....You are the brothers of the suffering Christ, and with Him, if you wish, you are saving the world." As the Latin American bishops would themselves reminded us only three years later at the Medellín Conference, the Church called for by Vatican II is not a Church "for" the poor, or even a Church "with" the poor but—in John XXIII's words—a Church *of* the poor. The poor, the sick, and suffering are not only the evangeli*zed*; they are the evangeli*zers*, the ones with and through whom Jesus Christ is saving the world.

The famous first lines of the Council's Pastoral Constitution on the Church in the Modern World (*Gaudium et Spes*) suggest a similar sentiment: "The joys and the hopes, the griefs and the anxieties of the men of this age, especially those who are poor or in any way afflicted, these are the joys and hopes, the griefs and anxieties of the followers of Christ."[3] These are "the signs of the times" which must inform the Church's activity in the world. In light of the above-mentioned statements of Popes John XXIII and Paul VI, which as prologue and conclusion framed the Council's discussions, the rationale grounding this opening sentence of *Gaudium et Spes* is clear. For, if "the Church wishes to be particularly the Church of the Poor" and if the poor "are the living and transparent image" of Jesus Christ in the world today, then the Christian's identification and solidarity with the poor and afflicted is not only an ethical imperative but, indeed, a *theological* imperative; i.e., a privileged criterion of Christian faith itself. "Was it not in order to respond to their appeal as God's privileged ones," ask the bishops, "that Christ came, even going as far as to identify himself with them?"[4] The Second Vatican Council thus planted the seeds of what, in later Catholic social teaching, would come to be known as "the preferential option for the poor." Indeed, it was with explicit reference to Vatican II that the Latin American bishops at Medellín (1968) and Puebla (1979) articulated this concept in the decades following the council. In the words of the *Catechism of the Catholic Church*: "Those who are oppressed by poverty are the object of *a preferential love* on the part of the Church which, since her origin and in spite of the failings of many of her members, has not ceased to work for their relief, defense, and liberation through numerous works of charity which remain indispensable always and everywhere."[5]

In order to understand the profound implications of Vatican II's "turn to the poor" for Catholic belief, social teaching, and theology, therefore, we should examine more closely the theological concept of a "preferential option for the poor" as well as the reasons why we Christians so often resist this concept, water it down, and blind ourselves to its practical demands. We should try to understand the internal logic of the option for the poor as deriving from the logic of Christian faith itself.

The preferential option for the poor is one of the most influential theological concepts of the last fifty years—and one of the most misunderstood. However, no sooner is the term mentioned than it is met with the rejoinder, "But what about the rich? Aren't we supposed to love them as well?" or "Why are the poor necessarily any better than the rich? Surely there are plenty of bad poor people!" or "I thought that Christians were supposed to be about harmony and reconciliation, not partiality and divisiveness."

The Peruvian theologian Gustavo Gutiérrez has suggested that the two principal, overarching themes in Scripture are: (1) the universality and gratuity of God's love, and (2) God's preferential love for the poor. In this paper, I will argue that these are two integrally-related, mutually implicit principles; i.e., that you can't have one without the other. More precisely, the universality and gratuity of God's love presupposes and demands God's preferential option for the poor and, conversely, the latter safeguards and guarantees the former. We, therefore, are called to participate in God's own preferential love for the poor, to make our own option for the poor—not primarily because of who the poor are but because of who God is, a God whose extravagant, boundless mercy exceeds all our preconceptions and expectations by embracing even the most seemingly unworthy among us. The liberation of the poor, therefore, is also God's own liberation from our clutches, from all our attempts to reduce divine Mystery to our own categories and calculi.

I will suggest, further, that the possibility of making such an option is impeded not so much by our fear of or hatred of "the other" as by our fundamental fear of and hatred of ourselves. Under the sway of what the social psychologist Ernest Becker famously called the "denial of death," we are unwilling to confront our own mortality and, by so doing, inflict death on others. If this is true, I will submit finally, the preferential option for the poor is a precondition not only for the liberation of God from our clutches but for our own liberation as First World Christians.

The rationality of God's option for the poor

God's preferential love for the poor is the theological and methodological guarantee, or safeguard, of God's transcendence, sovereignty, and Mystery. If God is truly "Other" and, thus, irreducible to any human concept or construction, then *logically* God will take the side of the poor, the marginalized, the outcast, the victim. In other words, *if* God loves everyone equally and gratuitously, *then* God will love the poor preferentially. What, at first glance, appear to be mutually contradictory assertions are, in fact, mutually implicit.

This conclusion can only be reached, however, if one first acknowledges that the poor *exist*, that there *are* people who exist on the margins of our society and world who are all but invisible to the rest of us. If there are indeed poor persons then, by definition, there are non-poor persons, since such terms as "poor," "marginalized," and "powerless" are inherently relative terms. Thus, the Jesuit theologian Jon Sobrino distinguishes between those persons who take life for granted and those who cannot take life for granted[6]—and the latter constitute two-thirds of the human family. In other words, those whom we deem "marginalized" or "excluded" are the vast majority of the global population. Tragically, we live in a divided world and society, and the persons in the best position to acknowledge that fact are those who suffer the consequences of the division. Conversely, that small minority of us who benefit—whether explicitly or implicitly—from social divisions are likely to either ignore these or deemphasize their significance. It is the hungry person who is in the best position to determine whether hunger

65

exists in our society. In Sobrino's terms, the person who cannot take life for granted is in the best position to be "honest about reality."[7] In other words, the poor or powerless have a privileged epistemological perspective from which to evaluate "reality." (Note, however, that such privilege in no way assumes infallibility or inevitability—only a greater likelihood of accuracy.)

If we do indeed live in a divided world in which the victims of that division have an epistemological privilege, then, what is the *theological* significance of this reality? More specifically, what can it mean to say that God enters into and becomes incarnate in a world, society, and history that are beset by divisions between those who have power (and take life for granted) and those who are powerless (and cannot take life for granted)? In such a world, what would it mean to say that God loves all people equally and gratuitously? In such a world, what would it mean to say that Jesus Christ is the perfect expression of God's love?

For two thousand years, the Christian tradition has proposed an answer that, for many, has seemed inconceivable, if not scandalous: in such a world the perfect expression of God's love is found in the utter powerlessness of a condemned criminal who, having experienced abandonment by his closest friends and even God, hangs pitiably from a cross. God's love enters history in the person of an outcast who is tortured and crucified for befriending other outcasts. God's love enters a divided society on the side of those who suffer the consequences of the division—not because God loves the outcast more but because in the midst of division and conflict God's love for the victims and God's love for their victimizers must take different forms. Indeed, God's love for the powerful will not (at least initially) be experienced as love at all, since it will take the form of challenge, confrontation, and a call to conversion, to *metanoia*.

To say that God's love is universal is not to say that it is *neutral*. In fact, it is to say the very opposite: precisely *because* God's love is universal, it *cannot* be neutral. If a mother finds that a fight has broken out between her strapping teenage son and his much smaller sister, the mother will not hesitate to try to "liberate" the smaller girl from the brother's clutches—precisely because the mother loves her two children equally. *In that context*, the mother's love for her son will take the form of a call to "conversion," though he will not likely see it that way. Were the mother to take a neutral stance and not get involved because she "loves her children equally," the young daughter would not experience the neutrality as love. In a situation of division, a neutral stance is implicit support for the divided status quo and, therefore, implicit support for the person(s) benefiting from the division; i.e., the most powerful. Neutrality, like silence, is consent.

The crucified and risen Christ is the historical incarnation of this logic, the logic of God's universal, gratuitous love. If the incarnate God is truly Other, truly Mystery, then God will be revealed most fully among those persons who themselves are most "other," most incomprehensible, in our world. The God who is absolutely Other and thus "makes no sense" in the context of merely human calculations and expectations will be encountered most fully among those persons whose very existence makes no sense; e.g., among the hungry in a gluttonous world, among the powerless in a power-mad world, among the insecure in a world obsessed with security—in Sobrino's words, among those who cannot take life for granted in a world that takes life for granted, and in Gutierrez's words, among the non-persons in a world that identifies personhood with wealth, power, and security. In the crucified Christ, God assumes the most degrading, dehumanizing dimensions of victimized human existence by becoming the absolute Victim. God does this not to privilege victimhood—which is always an evil—but precisely to reveal, once and for all, the absolutely gratuitous and universal character of God's love for *all* persons, indeed for all Creation.

The "denial of death"

In the remainder of this paper, I will propose that a fundamental obstacle to Christian faith, thus understood, is what Ernest Becker called the denial of death. To help make this argument I will begin with three anecdotes.

The first anecdote deals with my visit to Cuba several years ago, after the visit of Pope John Paul II to the same island. I was born in Cuba many years ago and left when I was only a young boy. I had not been able to return until many years later, when I returned under the auspices of a Church-related humanitarian mission. More than forty-five years had passed since I had last peered out an airplane window at the turquoise terminal building. It was exactly as I remembered it. So were the huge white block letters on the façade: *"Aeropuerto Internacional José Martí—La Habana"* (José Martí International Airport—Havana"). When I left, I was a six-year-old awaiting a flight to who-knows-where for who-knows-how-long. Together with my mother, grandmother, and siblings, I was leaving the only home I had ever known, escaping the increasingly violent, oppressive rule of a dictator. My father and grandfather were staying behind to care for my ninety-year-old great-grandmother, who was too old to fly. Through the impenetrable airplane window, I waved anxiously at them, not knowing if or when I would see them again. The scene would remain forever seared in my memory. That, in fact, is my earliest memory—looking out an airplane window, leaving my home, not knowing whether I would ever again see my father and grandfather.

Our family, thank God, was eventually reunited here in Miami. And now, more than four decades later, I myself was returning to be reunited with a land and a people that had given me birth. I had no idea how I, who had fled with my family and found success in the United States, would be received by the Cubans on the island. Like an orphan returning to meet his parents after forty-five years, I was deeply anxious. After all, during those four decades the people of Cuba and the Cuban exile community in the United States had seemingly become estranged. Even as many Cuban-Americans had achieved economic and political success in the United States, the Cubans who had remained on the island had been suffering from unimaginable poverty and political oppression. How would the impoverished, beaten-down Cuban people who struggled to survive in such desperate circumstances, receive me, who had been fortunate enough to flee with his family? Would they resent me? Would they feel that I, along with the other hundreds of thousands of Cuban exiles, had abandoned them to their plight?

It didn't take long for my fears to be assuaged. Wherever I went on the island, the Cuban people's response to my visit was the same: "Thank you for not forgetting us; thank you for remembering us." I, who in some very real sense had abandoned them, was now being welcomed back with open arms, no questions asked—not with a "how dare you" but with a "thank you." Everywhere I went, the message I received was the same: "You are one of us; welcome back."

The second anecdote I'd like to share with you occurred when I was a college student. The sight of homeless persons asking for spare change was a common one on the streets immediately surrounding the campus where I went to school. Walking those streets at night in search of a sub at a local restaurant or a movie at a cinema, I would regularly come across a homeless man or woman, reach into my pocket, and place a couple of coins in his or her hand. It made me feel good. One particular evening, I happened upon a stocky, scruffy-looking, middle-aged homeless man standing on a street corner. As I approached him, he looked at me straight in the eye and asked for money. Perfunctorily, I reached into my pants pocket for loose change and placed the coins in his hand. After putting the money away, he came towards me with both arms outstretched and reached to grab my head. My heart stopped. As a well-educated young man with the self-assurance such young men so often have, I had always assumed I had risen above any petty bigotry or prejudices I may have harbored as a child. Yet at this moment I became numb with fear, fully expecting that I was about to be mugged. The scruffy homeless man did indeed grab my head. He put both hands on my forehead, as if to extend a blessing, and said, calmly, "Thank you. God bless you."

I walked away in a daze, trying to process what had just transpired, both the man's actions and my own instinctive reaction. I had a profound sense of both gratitude and shame. By the time I had composed myself and returned to the street corner to thank him for what he had done for me, he was already gone. For weeks later, I returned to that street corner hoping to see him so that I could thank *him*. I never saw him again.

My third anecdote concerns a friend of our family who lives in Chicago. She had worked as a nurse for several years in the emergency room of Cook County Hospital, a huge public hospital in the inner city. There she would regularly have to deal with the tragic human consequences of urban violence, ministering to hundreds of teenagers who had been victims of street gang gunfire.

69

After a while, our friend couldn't take it anymore. She became burnt out from the emotional intensity of constantly seeing so much pain and death, especially among young adolescents. So she left her job at Cook County Hospital for another nursing position, this one in a suburban hospital, in a much more well-to-do neighborhood. A couple of years later I was again talking with her, expecting to hear that her work was going much better, now that she was in a more peaceful environment. No, she told me, it's not necessarily more peaceful in the suburbs. In fact, she said, I'm still extracting bullets from young kids' bodies. I still see lots of gunshot victims in the emergency room. The only difference is that *these* gunshot wounds are self-inflicted. These young men and women lived in leafy neighborhoods with row upon row of large houses with well-manicured lawns; they attended the finest schools; they seemingly had everything they could possible want, everything we're told will make us happy. Yet, for some reason, some of these model teenagers were living in such desperation that they were driven to take their own lives. How could this be, I asked myself. I later learned that, if the highest rates of teenage homicides are in our urban ghettoes, the highest rates of teen suicide are in our suburbs.

You might ask what these three stories—seemingly so different—have in common. Rather than ask such an abstract question, however, what I'd like to do is ask the more personal question, what did *I* learn from these experiences? So let me share with you some reflections. An important lesson I learned from these three experiences is that I crave security; I don't like to feel like I'm not in control of my own life. I want to make sure that my life is all planned out and that nothing happens that I haven't foreseen. What makes me happy at the end of the day is the feeling that I've accomplished everything I set out to do that day and that nothing unexpected interrupted my plans. We want to know where we'll be five, ten, twenty years from now and we want to have control of our future: where we'll live, what job we'll have (whether we'll even have a job), who we'll marry, how many kids we'll have, when we'll retire, where we'll retire, etc., etc. This is especially true in our U.S. culture, where we're taught from the time we're small kids that, if we only strive and work hard enough, we can be in complete control of our lives; happiness means having a large enough bank account or an impressive enough résumé so that we never have to know what it's like to be insecure, to be vulnerable, to be out of control, to be powerless. During our current economic crisis, many people who had become accustomed to taking for granted their own security and that of their families are, for the first time in their lives, confronting such a painful loss of control, a sense of powerlessness or vulnerability in the face of life's uncertainties.

Yet to be a human being, to be alive, is to exist in a situation of inherent insecurity, vulnerability, and uncertainty. Regardless of how much money we have, where we go to college, or how prestigious our job is, we do not know and cannot know what tomorrow holds. But we try to avoid this painful lesson at all costs. One way we do this is by avoiding those people in our communities who themselves live in situations of vulnerability, powerlessness, and insecurity. We thus erect all sorts of walls and barriers, both visible and invisible, to protect and shield us from the most vulnerable people of our societies: the poor, the sick, the elderly, the homeless, the stranger, the alien, the downtrodden. We feel threatened by them because they remind us of what we'd rather forget: namely, that ultimately we're all in the same boat; none of us is in complete control; none of us knows for sure what the future holds. We avoid the poor, the homeless, and the destitute not because we're afraid of *them* but because we're afraid of *ourselves;* we're afraid that we may not be as secure as we think we are. The lives of the vulnerable, powerless people of our society are the mirrors of our own souls. So we put them out of sight: in ghettoes, on the other side of the tracks, on the other side of the border, in shelters and institutions where we'll never have to come across them. We put them anywhere but in our secure, peaceful neighborhoods.

The Christian story represents a fundamental rejection of this dynamic of exclusion and violence. After their friend's crucifixion, Jesus' disciples themselves sought the illusory security of four walls, secluding themselves in the upper room out of fear for their lives. But into that room irrupts unexpectedly the resurrected Victim, who invites them to look at his wounds. They must have been terrified of those wounds, the wounds on the body of the Victim whom they had helped crucify by abandoning him on the way to Calvary. No wonder the disciples were frightened! Indeed, they must have been scared to death at the sight of the man they had just betrayed, who was now confronting them with the very visible, concrete signs of that betrayal—those irksome wounds. The disciples had probably assumed that, now that Jesus was dead, they could put the past behind them, chalk it up to a misguided idealism, and go on to live the contented lives of good, upstanding fishermen, tax collectors, etc. However, in walks Jesus unexpectedly to remind them of that troubling past, to prick consciences that had just begun to find some equilibrium, however tenuous. In the upper room, Jesus reveals to the disciples not only who *he* is but also who *they* are, and he does this by sticking his wounds in their faces! He doesn't say "let bygones be bygones," or "forgive and forget." Instead, he refuses to allow his disciples to forget what they had done to him. Jesus forces them to confront the painful consequences of their abandonment and betrayal: "Look and see…," put your hand here, do *not* forget what you have done to me! Yet Jesus does this not to condemn his friends—which must surely be what they had expected—but to forgive them, to extend an unexpected mercy to them, to liberate them from their fears and anxieties. As he shows them his wounds, he says to them, "Peace be with you," and sits down to break bread with them. He forgives by *not* forgetting.

It is only when the disciples are confronted by the innocent Victim who unexpectedly irrupts into their secure world that they are forced to confront their own weakness and are thus liberated from their fear. It is only then that they can acknowledge their dependence on the Victim for their own well-being. It is only then that Thomas has the courage to proclaim "My Lord and my God!" The refusal to face the wounds that appear on Christ's resurrected body and on the bodies of all the victims of history, those whom Sobrino calls the "Crucified People," is *the* mortal sin (in the most literal sense of the term), for it leads inevitably to the death of others and, indeed, to our own death.

The murderous consequences of this "denial of death" in contemporary Western societies were examined over a quarter century ago by Becker, who argued that the anxiety and, even, terror that we experience in the face of our own fundamental vulnerability and mortality is the foundational experience around which we construct our Selves and our societies.[8] This need to deny our mortality, our ultimate powerlessness in the face of death, is what drives us to construct personal identities, social institutions, ideologies, and belief systems that can make us feel invulnerable and ultimately invincible. To be a human being is to exist in a state of the most profound vulnerability and contingency; our lives are ultimately not in our control, for they can be extinguished at any moment. But we cannot bear this fact. So we construct a world that will shield us from this terrifying truth. Invariably, however, we eventually discover that the world we construct in order to shield us from our own mortality and powerlessness has resulted in the very opposite; it is a world that fosters death in all its forms. What Becker details is precisely the process by which the individual strives to exempt him- or herself from the common lot of all persons, our common mortality. And that process ultimately deals death, to the "others" against whom the individual must assert his or her singular invulnerability, and death to the individual him or herself, since the need to presume oneself invulnerable leads to total isolation: from other persons, from God, and even from oneself.

In the language of social psychology, Becker thus articulates the consequences of erasing, ignoring, or failing to acknowledge the wounds on the risen body of Christ—the consequences of interpreting the resurrection apart from its concrete history, which includes the abandonment signaled by the crowing cock as well as the wounds resulting from that abandonment. Those consequences are always horrific. Becker argues that the corollary of our obsessive need to feel invulnerable in the face of our mortality is the need to avoid all pain, all suffering, for these appear in our lives as unwanted reminders that we are not in control of our own lives, that we are indeed vulnerable. If death is the ultimate enemy, the ultimate threat to our sense of security and invulnerability, so too are all those partial deaths that foreshadow our common end: illness, old age, poverty, failure, abandonment. So these must be avoided at all costs. Indeed, our consumer culture is premised on and driven by the promise that all these forms of human vulnerability are avoidable if we have the right kind of insurance, the latest model automobile, or the most fashionable wardrobe. Likewise, authentic human relationships of mutual love and trust are to be shunned, since these always involve a dimension of vulnerability and even pain in the face of an "other" who, however much we may seek to control, always remains beyond our control; if one "falls" in love, one might "get burned." So we surround ourselves with "things" that promise security and invulnerability, and we run from "persons," since these will demand vulnerability and the possibility of pain. We fall in love with cars, houses, mobile phones, and computers even as we remain unattached to human persons.

But not just any persons—weak, powerless, vulnerable persons in particular. Wounded persons. It is these who are especially threatening to our sense of invulnerability. It is these who are the mirrors of our own souls, whose very existence threatens our sense of invulnerability, security, and control. What I feared about that homeless man who confronted me on a street corner was simply the fact that he was there, the fact that he confronted me and, in doing so, forced me to recognize my connection to him and to his predicament. And that was terrifying.

In fact, the very existence of the wounded in our midst is so terrifying that we must eradicate them or, at least, hide them from view, "get them off the streets"—so that we won't have to see them and their uncomfortable wounds. So, argues Becker, the violence inflicted on the weak among us, from the Jews in Nazi concentration camps to the children left to die in the poverty of our contemporary concentration camps, the ghettoes of Western cities and Third World rural villages, is simply the social face of the denial of death. If we deny death we inflict it. But we also inflict it on ourselves. The fear of pain and vulnerability that causes us to shun real human relationships, to shun that true love that always involves surrender and vulnerability in the face of an "other," ultimately kills our interior life, our ability to feel anything—neither pain nor joy, nor love. For, as psychologists remind us, if we repress painful feelings out of fear, we will instinctively also repress any positive feelings; we cannot pick and choose which feelings to repress. To repress all feelings of insecurity or pain out of fear is to make joy and love impossible. So we succumb to every kind of addiction, we crave any kind of anesthetic that will make us numb to our inner life, so that we won't have to feel anything.

The result of this pathological fear of our own fragility as human beings is the despair and hopelessness that lies just beneath the surface of our most "successful" communities and families. To scratch that well-manicured surface is to discover the silent desperation that manifests itself in a myriad of self-destructive ways, from chronic depression, to every conceivable form of addiction, to destroyed and destructive relationships, to suicide itself—simply the literal expression of the internal suicide we have already committed when we wall ourselves off from others and, therefore, from ourselves. Thus, the suicide rate among suburban white males—the highest for any demographic group—is simply the corollary of the murder rate among inner city African American and Latino males. The former is a direct result of our failure to confront the latter.

The most threatening "others" are precisely those who are the weakest, most powerless and fragile, for these represent the repressed, dangerous memory of our *common* mortality. There is thus a direct, intimate relationship between the struggle for social justice and the possibility of authentic Christian faith and worship, the expression of gratitude for a life that is not ours but is pure gift. The act of solidarity with the wounded "other" is, at the same time, an acknowledgment of our common woundedness, our common powerlessness. It is also an acknowledgment of our complicity in the infliction of those wounds. That is why we tragically continue to erect geographical, social, cultural, racial, economic, and psychological barriers between ourselves and "them," so that we will not have to face "them", and thus face *ourselves.* So we avoid touching— or even seeing—the wounds. We avoid risking the act of solidarity, or companionship with the victims of history.

Yet once in a while the apparent peace of this environment is shattered; once in a while one of the very people we spend our lives avoiding dares to breech the emotional or geographical barriers we've set up, irrupting into our world and disrupting our security. The crucified victim whom we had abandoned out of fear for our lives irrupts into the upper room and, instead of condemning us, says" "Peace be with you..." The old, beleaguered Cuban lady embraces me to thank me for "not forgetting" her, or the homeless man extends his arms to bless and thank me, in both cases breaking through the thick wall of fear I had erected to protect me from them.

But what about that nurse in Chicago? What did I learn from her? I learned to look deep into my own heart, my own life, and my own community to see whether, below the placid surface, some of us might not be leading what Henry David Thoreau called "lives of quiet desperation." Behind those clean, white picket fences one may indeed find loving, happy families and communities. But maybe if we look carefully enough, if we scratch the well-scrubbed surface, we'll also find families bereft of mutual love and respect, broken relationships, addictions of every sort, and even violence. More importantly, that nurse taught me to ask the question: Is there a relationship, a connection between the overt violence of our inner cities and the much less obvious, though equally destructive violence of our most well-to-do communities? Maybe, just maybe, the fear of vulnerability that has driven us into communities isolated geographically, emotionally, and spiritually from the people "on the other side of the tracks" has had unintended consequences; maybe that same fear of vulnerability ultimately isolates us from the persons closest to us and even isolates us from our very selves. If to be a human being is to live in vulnerability, then to fear vulnerability is to fear life itself. Indeed, it is to be incapable of real human relationships, for a relationship demands that I place myself before another human being in a situation of deepest vulnerability, never knowing for sure how that person will react to my overtures of friendship. The fear of insecurity that demands ever larger bank accounts and insurance policies, that erects ever higher walls and installs ever more sophisticated alarm systems, is the same fear that numbs us to our deepest needs and feelings, anesthetizes us to our deepest desire to be loved and to love. Ultimately, if we're afraid to feel vulnerable, we'll be afraid to feel anything at all, including love.

And this implies that, in the end, our own happiness is itself beyond our control—whatever advertisers and marketers may try to tell us. Happiness is not a "thing" that we can grasp and possess. Those who think it is will spend their lives in anxiety and fear; anxiety until they attain happiness, and, were they to attain what they think is happiness, fear lest they lose it. Happiness can be neither sought nor bought. This belief is at the heart of Christ's message: "For those who want to save their life will lose it; and those who lose their life for my sake will find it" (Matt 16:25). Christ does not call us to pursue happiness but risk vulnerability, to reach across the many borders and barriers we've erected to separate "us" from "them," to separate those who are "like us" from those who are "different."

If we do so, if we dare to breech the borders that divide us, we might discover the real secret of happiness, namely, that happiness is not a goal to be attained but a gift to be received. Like any true gift, we're not in control of who offers it or when they offer it. So the more obsessively we pursue our own happiness, and the more tightly we grasp onto our own idea of what constitutes happiness, the more closed we will become to the unexpected kiss on the forehead or the grateful embrace that breaks through our protective barriers as if from another world. For, very often, the persons bearing that gift are precisely the poor, the strangers, the weak, the powerless—in other words, precisely those persons whom we expect to be the most depressed and *un*happy. And so, in our pursuit of happiness, we avoid them.

However, just when we think we've got our lives figured out and planned out, something happens that surprises us, takes us aback, turns our world around, and makes us rethink all those previous assumptions. What happens is simply life itself, life as the gratuitous gift of a God whose mercy refuses to be walled in. As John Lennon wrote, "Life is what happens when you're busy making other plans." Life is what happened to me as I planned my visit to Cuba anxiously preparing myself for the resentful feelings I was sure I'd encounter. Life is what happened to me that evening as I walked along a college campus looking only for a sandwich. Yes, make plans, but always remain open to people and experiences that might alter your plans. Life is what happens when you come to the wholly unexpected realization that "we are mortal, frail human beings"—*all* of us, whether we like it or not. At bottom, a life is not something achieved but a gift received. Therein lies the beginning of humility and true happiness. No, we're not in control. Someone else is. That knowledge is the source of true joy, true happiness.

So, in the end, our preferential option for the poor is but the acknowledgement of our common contingency, our common dependence on a God whose mercy exceeds all our limits and expectations. This is what the bishops at the Second Vatican Council meant when they called the poor "God's privileged ones." When one chooses to stand alongside the poor, one will certainly discover that many, many poor persons lead extraordinary, inspiring lives of deep faith and invincible courage in the face of unimaginable hardships. Yet the poor are privileged, not because *they're* necessarily good, but because *God* is good. They're privileged because they are the witnesses to a God whose love knows no borders, no boundaries, not barriers. They're privileged because the liberation of the poor is the precondition for our own liberation and, most importantly, the precondition for God's own liberation.

*Portions of this paper have appeared in my book *Christ Our Companion: Toward a Theological Aesthetics of Liberation* (Maryknoll, NY: Orbis Books, 2009) and my essay "The Preferential Option for the Poor: Christ and the Logic of Gratuity," in Robert Lassalle-Klein, ed., *Jesus of Galilee: Contextual Christology for the 21st Century* (Maryknoll, NY: Orbis Books, 2011).

Dr. Roberto S. Goizueta *is the Margaret O'Brien Flatley Professor of Catholic Theology at Boston College in Chestnut Hill, MA.*

DISCUSSION QUESTIONS

1. What is the role of Catholic universities in promoting a "preferential option for the poor"? In what concrete ways might Catholic universities embody and promote such an option? What are the institutional and social obstacles that universities would face?
2. What is the role of the Church in promoting a preferential option for the poor? In what concrete ways might the Church embody and promote such an option? What are the institutional and social obstacles that the Church faces?
3. What are some concrete examples of how I succumb to a "denial of death" in my own life? What are the consequences of this behavior for my life, the lives of my family and friends, and the lives of the poor?
4. When and where has my life been touched and changed unexpectedly by an encounter with "the poor, the sick, and suffering"?

SUGGESTED READINGS

Daniel G. Groody, ed. *The Option for the Poor in Christian Theology*. South Bend, IN: University of Notre Dame Press, 2007.

Gustavo Gutiérrez. *Spiritual Writings*. Maryknoll, NY: Orbis Books, 2011.

Thomas Massaro. *Living Justice: Catholic Social Teaching in Action*. Lanham, MD: Rowman and Littlefield, 2011.

David J. O'Brien and Thomas A. Shannon, eds. *Catholic Social Thought: The Documentary Heritage* [Updated/Expanded Edition]. Maryknoll, NY: Orbis Books, 2010.

NOTES

1. John XXIII, Radio message inaugurating the Second Vatican Council, September 11, 1962.

2. Paul VI, Address to the Poor, the Sick and the Suffering, December 8, 1965.

3. Vatican II, "Pastoral Constitution on the Church in the Modern World *Gaudium et Spes*," 1965, para. 1.

4. Vatican II, "Apostolic Exhortation on the Renewal of Religious Life," 17.

5. *Catechism of the Catholic Church*, no. 2448.

6. Jon Sobrino, *Jesus the Liberator* (Maryknoll, NY: Orbis Books, 1993), 85.

7. Jon Sobrino, *Spirituality of Liberation* (Maryknoll, NY: Orbis Books, 1988), 14–16.

8. Ernest Becker, *The Denial of Death* (New York: Free Press, 1973).

To Artists

A Reflection

Michael J. Himes

The Second Vatican Council's brief address to artists was welcome
—certainly it would have been a grievous omission not to address
them—but unclear both about what artists do and why they are
important to the Church. It described artists as people "who are
taken up with beauty and work for it," and came perilously close to
trivializing art as a catechetical aid "translating [the Church's]
divine message in the language of forms and figures." It invoked
the longstanding alliance between Church leaders and artists who
"have built and adorned [the church's] temples, celebrated her dog-
mas, enriched her liturgy." This is all well and good so far as it goes,
but it reduces art to an educational tool or a religious decoration. I
suggest that art has a much deeper, much richer, and absolutely
essential connection with the Church's proclamation.

 The Council's message to artists describes them as centrally
concerned with beauty. But what does that mean? Like "truth" and
"goodness," beauty names something undeniably necessary in
human experience but notoriously hard to describe. To do so, I turn
to James Joyce who in the final section of his novel *A Portrait of the
Artist as a Young Man* gives a rich exploration of beauty. It may seem
unusual for a theologian to invoke Joyce as an aid in making his
case but surely not more so than for a novelist to invoke Thomas
Aquinas in making his, which is what Joyce does when the protag-
onist of his novel, Stephen Daedalus, tries to explain to his friend
Lynch what beauty is as they stroll about Dublin. Although Joyce
depicts his young hero as somewhat pretentious in the solemnity of
his explanation, the conversation between Stephen and Lynch is

central to Joyce 's understanding of himself as an artist. Stephen refers his friend to a quotation from Thomas Aquinas: *ad pulchritudinem tria requiruntur: integritas, consonantia, claritas.*

> Stephen pointed to a basket which a butcher's boy had slung inverted on his head.
> —Look at that basket—he said.
> —I see it—said Lynch.
> —In order to see that basket—said Stephen—your mind first of all separates the basket from the rest of the visible universe which is not the basket. The first phase of apprehension is a bounding line drawn about the object to be apprehended. An esthetic image is presented to us either in space or in time. What is audible is presented in time, what is visible is presented in space. But, temporal or spatial, the esthetic image is first luminously apprehended as selfbounded and self contained upon the immeasurable background of space or time which is not it. You apprehend it as one thing. You see it as one whole. You apprehend its wholeness. That is *integritas.*
> —Bull's eye!—said Lynch, laughing—Go on.[1]

The first step in apprehending something as beautiful is to see it as a single and unique event. The picture frame is an underappreciated advance in the development of the visual arts. Without a frame, the boundaries of a painter's work would be the space available. The size and shape of the wall would determine the size and shape of the painting. If the wall included a door or a window, or if it had irregular planes or angles, these features would have to be incorporated into the painting. But by framing a canvas an artist can determine the space to which the viewer should attend. The picture-frame is a convention, a tacit agreement between the artist and the viewer by which they agree that a certain space will occupy their attention and that everything else is to be bracketed. A similar conventional exclusion occurs in time as well as space. After the sounds of the orchestra tuning cease, when the conductor raises the baton and stands poised at the podium for an instant before the music begins, the music is framed by silence. During the concert we may hear late-comers arrive, someone cough, or a chair creak, but we recognize such noises as distractions, not parts of the music. We hear them, but we know that we are not to attend to them. In an encounter with any artwork, certain sense impressions are ruled in and others are ruled out. This is the effect of the "bounding line" drawn around the work.

—Then—said Stephen—you pass from point to point, led by its formal lines; you apprehend it as balanced part against part within its limits; you feel the rhythm of its structure. In other words the synthesis of immediate perception is followed by the analysis of apprehension. Having first felt that it is one thing you feel now that it is a thing. You apprehend it as complex, multiple, divisible, separable, made up of its parts, the result of its parts and their sum, harmonious. That is *consonantia*.
—Bull's eye again!—said Lynch wittily.—Tell me now what is *claritas* and you win the cigar.[2]

Claritas refers to the internal harmony of that which is bounded in time or space, that to which we agree to attend. Consider the difference between being interested in a particular painting and decorating a room. In the first case, the question of whether the colors of the painting or its size and shape clash with the decor of the room in which the painting is displayed is irrelevant. In the second, whether the painting "fits" with the rest of the room's furnishings is of great concern. Is the canvas or the room the unit to which we attend? It may legitimately be either. If it is the room, then we may be interested in whether the colors in the painting blend with the drapes and the carpet and the furniture. In that case the painting is experienced not as a work in itself but as item of furniture in the room. It is the *consonantia*, the harmony of the room which is of central concern. But if the painting itself is the object of our attention, then whether it "fits" with the rest of the room is beside the point. After determining the unit to which we attend, i.e., after acknowledging the *integritas* of the object which arrests our attention, then we notice how the parts, the colors, shapes, forms, textures, within that unit work with one another.

But the most difficult and important of the three qualities of beauty remains: *claritas*.

—The connotation of the word—Stephen said—is rather vague. Aquinas uses a term which seems to be inexact. It baffled me for a long time. It would lead you to believe that he had in mind symbolism or idealism, the supreme quality of beauty being a light from some other world, the idea of which the matter is but a shadow, the reality of which it is but the symbol. I thought that he might mean that *claritas* is the artistic discovery and representation of the divine purpose in anything or a force of generalization which would make the esthetic image a universal one, make it outshine its proper conditions. But that is literary talk. I understand it so. When you have apprehended that basket as one thing and have then analysed it according to its form and apprehended it as a thing you make the only synthesis which is logically and esthetically permissible. You see that it is that thing which it is and no other thing. The radiance of which he speaks is the scholastic *quidditas,* the "whatness" of a thing. This supreme quality is felt by the artist when the esthetic image is first conceived in his imagination. The mind in that mysterious instant Shelley likened beautifully to a fading coal. The instant wherein that supreme quality of beauty, the clear radiance of the esthetic image, is apprehended luminously by the mind which has been arrested by its wholeness and fascinated by its harmony is the luminous silent stasis of esthetic pleasure, a spiritual state very like to that cardiac condition which the Italian physiologist Luigi Galvani, using a phrase almost as beautiful as Shelley's, called the enchantment of the heart.[3]

The image that Joyce quotes from Shelley, that the object in the mind's eye of the artist is like a fading coal, is very helpful in grasping his meaning. As the flames die down in a fireplace and only glowing embers are left, the light comes from within the coals or the remnants of the logs. That is the point of Shelley's image: the coal is lit from within. Joyce refers to *quidditas.* Although the discussion on beauty began with a quotation from Thomas, *quidditas* is a term associated more with Scotus. As Joyce employs it in this passage, "*quidditas*" may best be understood by reference to another master of the English language who was deeply influenced by Scotus, Gerard Manley Hopkins. In his sonnet, "As Kingfishers Catch Fire," Hopkins wrote:

> Each mortal thing does one thing and the same:
> Deals out that being indoors each one dwells;
> Selves—goes itself; myself it speaks and spells,
> Crying What I do is me: for that I came.[4]

Notice that wonderful use of "self" as a verb. Each thing "does one thing and the same": it "selves." The task of each thing that exists is to be that particular thing and not anything else. The *quidditas* of a thing is its "selving"; it is a thing being what it is. This is what Joyce/Stephen Daedalus presents as the preeminent quality of something beautiful: it is what it is, and it is not anything else. It is uniquely itself. A beautiful object does not point the viewer to anything else. It points to itself. It "selves," it "goes itself," it "deals out that being" that dwells within it. It ex-presses itself; it impels itself outward in all directions.

The key point to notice is that a beautiful work—whether painting or poem, statue or piece of music, dance or building—does not point us outward to something else; it draws us within itself. The preeminent "task" of the work of art is to catch our attention. To make us notice it. The chief effect of a work of beauty is to make us notice it, not to point us "beyond" itself to something else. Goethe, who certainly knew something about beauty and art, maintained that this "drawing in" as contrasted with "pointing outward" is the very essence of an artwork.

> There is a great difference, whether the poet seeks the particular for the general or sees the general in the particular. From the first procedure arises allegory, where the particular serves only as an example of the general; the second procedure, however, is really the nature of poetry: it expresses something particular without thinking of the general or pointing to it. True symbolism is where the particular represents the more general, not as a dream or a shadow, but as a living momentary revelation of the Inscrutable.[5]

So the first and most important effect of a beautiful work of art is to impinge on our awareness, to demand our attention, to make us notice it. And it is here that the work of the artist and the mission of the church coincide. To explain how and why this is true it will be useful to consider the sacramental principle: that which is always and everywhere true must be noticed, accepted, and celebrated somewhere, sometime. What is constantly present is frequently ignored. We do not usually think about the oxygen in a room until its exhaustion forces us to notice it. Our hearts beat continually, but we do not think about the action of our hearts – unless failure of their action demands our attention. Our experience is full of instances of this principle: an omnipresent reality tends to lose its reality. But the Christian tradition, especially in its Catholic form, maintains that the love of God is omnipresent. Everything that exists does so because it is loved by God. Why does anything exist? Why is there something rather than nothing? The answer offered by Christianity is that God freely loves into being everything that is. God does not need the existence of anything else because God, after all, is God. If anything exists that is not God (i.e., the universe), it does not exist in order to give God anything, to meet some need or supply some lack in God. Rather, the universe (i.e., you and I and everything else that is but is not God) exists in order that God may give something to it. There are, then, two possibilities: either God gives the universe something other than Godself—but that would simply be more of the universe—or God gives Godself. The reason that there is something rather than nothing, the foundation of existence, is the self-giving of God. The Christian answer to the question why something exists is that God loves it into being. The word long employed in the Christian tradition to name the self-giving of God that is the ground of creation as a whole and of every creature individually is *grace*.

Grace is omnipresent. Anything and everything that exists rests on grace. But if grace is omnipresent, then grace is likely to be unnoticed. In accord with the sacramental principle, grace, the self-gift of God, must be noticed, accepted, and celebrated somewhere sometime. Any person, place, thing, or event, any sight, sound, taste, touch, or smell that causes us to attend to the grace that lies at the roots of all that exists, to say "yes" to it, and to gratefully celebrate it, is a sacrament. In our Catholic tradition, of course, there are the seven great communal sacraments. All of us, however, have in our lives particular persons and experiences that powerfully and effectively cause us to become aware of the grace that grounds our being constantly.

Hopkins gave beautiful expression to the sacramental principle in his poem "Hurrahing in Harvest." The poet stops bemoaning the passing of summer and the onset of winter when he notices the beauties and joys unique to the autumn and to which he had previously been inattentive, and he writes: "These things, these things were here and but the beholder / Wanting."[6] Grace is omnipresent; what, too often, is wanting is someone to notice it, a beholder. Indeed, the central purpose of Catholic tradition is to form us as beholders. In a paper written in the early years of the twentieth century, Friedrich von Hügel cited Charles Darwin as a striking example of authentic asceticism, disciplining oneself so that one can see *what is there*, not what one hopes or wishes or fears might be there. For Darwin subordinated his extraordinary energy, knowledge, patience, and perseverance to painstaking observation of varying forms "of fly-trap plants and of orchids, of earthworms and of humming-birds." "He was always loving, learning, watching; he was always 'out of himself,' doubling himself up, as it were, so as to penetrate these realities so much lowlier than himself, so different from himself."[7] Von Hügel knew that asceticism is part of the training needed to become a beholder.

The artwork, like the sacrament, demands that we attend, that we see what is there to be seen. The first effect of a work of art in any field is to cause us to attend to what is there before us. The artist tries to see what is there to be seen and through his poem, play, music, dance, painting or sculpture to help us to attend more richly and deeply to the reality of things. The artist does this by expressing the very essence of things—the *this-ness* of things—so we see this thing, not another thing. The mistake is to think of a work of art in any medium as an incitement to think of something else, a signal pointing elsewhere. A work of art, like a sacrament, does not signify what is absent; it reveals what is present. It is not a reminder of what is missing; it is the uncovering of what is always with us. This is why the work of the artist is so closely connected to the mission of the Church. It is not that artists design and adorn our places of worship, or that they set our sacred texts to music or write about specifically religious themes. They are not auxiliaries in the work of religious education. If seeing things as they are, if learning to attend to what is there, is the essential step in becoming a sacramental beholder, then the Council Fathers were perhaps even more right than they knew when they declared fifty years ago that if you are friends of genuine art, you are our friends.

Rev. Michael J. Himes *is Professor of Theology at Boston College in Chestnut Hill, MA.*

DISCUSSION QUESTIONS

1. If there is a real connection between creating or appreciating a work of art and participating in the sacramental life of the Church, have you experienced that in your church communities? How might the connection be made within our communities?
2. Do you find James Joyce's (and St. Thomas Aquinas's) description of the three requirements for beauty to be true of your experience of beauty?
3. How do you relate the many personal sacraments that we all have as individuals to the seven public and communal sacraments of the Church?

SUGGESTED READINGS

Nicholas Boyle. *Sacred and Secular Scriptures: A Catholic Approach to Literature*. South Bend IN: University of Notre Dame Press, 2005.

Bernard Cooke. *Sacraments and Sacramentality*. Mystic CT: Twenty-Third Publications, 1983.

Nicholas Lash. *Believing Three Ways in One God: A Reading of the Apostles' Creed*. South Bend IN: University of Notre Dame Press, 1993.

NOTES

1. James Joyce, *A Portrait of the Artist as a Young Man* (New York: Random House/The Modern Library, 1925), 249f.

2. Joyce, *A Portrait of the Artist as a Young Man*, 249.

3. Joyce, *A Portrait of the Artist as a Young Man*, 249f.

4. W. H. Gardner and N. H. MacKenzie, eds., *The Poems of Gerard Manley Hopkins* (London: Oxford University Press, 1967, 4th ed.), 90.

5. Johann Wolfgang von Goethe, *Maximen*, 1:211, trans. by René Wellek.

6. *Poems of Gerard Manley Hopkins*, 70.

7. Baron Friedrich von Hügel, *Essays and Addresses on the Philosophy of Religion*, First Series (London: J. M. Dent and Sons Ltd., 1921), 103.

To Youth

Sarah L. Heiman and Peter Denio

Introduction

Fifty years after the beginning of the first session of the Second Vatican Council and almost forty-seven years after its address to youth, one might have expected the youth of the world would be different. Yet the nature of the drastic changes affecting young people in 2012 may have been beyond most people's imagination when compared to the youth of the early and mid-1960's. If a message to youth were drafted today it would clearly differ from the one at the end of the Second Vatican Council; much has changed in the intervening years. At the same time many of the concerns expressed in the address persist today and may, in fact, have become even more prevalent. New realities, due to a new digital revolution and a generation that has been ever more shaped by postmodernism, offer new opportunities and challenges unimagined by the bishops as they addressed the youth in 1965. Even the development of the address would likely be more collaborative—not only among the bishops but also involving the youth in its preparation. While these differences are important to note, the preparations, work, and writings of the Second Vatican Council exhibit a Church capable of relating to and engaging young people. This capability will be examined through an exploration of the context in which the message was crafted and delivered so that we may better understand the intention of the address. With this context in mind we will consider the world that this current generation of youth has inherited as it compares and contrasts to the setting in which the message was first given, and we will then conclude by reflecting on what would need to be addressed and understood if a message was issued today.

Before we undertake this analysis, however, it will be helpful to properly define the subject of our reflection. When we think of "youth" today many wonderfully contrasting and vibrant images come to mind. Consider the recent "Arab Spring," which was due in large part to the "youth bulge" in many Middle East countries; the fervent faith found in many African nations with populations that skew greatly toward young people; the challenges the Church faces in reaching young people in a context that is monitored and controlled by the state in China; the complexities of evangelizing young people in countries in South America where evangelical traditions are on the rise; or the experience in Europe where secularism has a strong hold on the population. These global realities provide a fascinating backdrop for our exploration of the experiences of youth in the United States and what the message to youth may have to say to them in particular. This emphasis will allow us to explore the message in light of our own personal experiences and ministerial milieu.

When discussing the youth of the United States we first need to be clear that, contrary to standard usage, children and adolescents are not the "youth" the bishops had in mind when they drafted the address to the youth, nor are they the youth we reference in this chapter. Instead, "youth" refers to young adults, identified by the United States Conference of Catholic Bishops today as "people in their late teens, twenties, and thirties," and often referred to as Millennials or Generation Next. While certain trends may be identified for any generation, individual young adults will differ greatly in terms of their faith commitment, living situations, political affiliations, and on almost any other indicator upon which they may be assessed.

In the address to youth, the bishops provide an outline for what the greatest qualities of a typical youth may be: "the ability to rejoice with what is beginning, to give oneself unreservedly, to renew one's self and to set out again for new conquests."[1] These characteristics, namely, enthusiasm, the ability to readily reform their behaviors and thinking, an indomitable spirit, and wholehearted generosity are qualities that should be celebrated and valued. Interestingly, the spirit of youth espoused seems to resonate across the boundaries of time, culture, religion, and race; although the social milieu in which young adults live may have changed, the esteemed qualities of youth remain constant.

Having briefly identified the parameters of the youth we will be discussing in this chapter we will now explore the Second Vatican Council's address to youth. The address to youth, shaped by the experience of Vatican II, informs how the Church can engage the youth of today to faithfully confront the challenges of the world around them and in the future. Our analysis begins with a review of the context in which the message was developed and proclaimed.

Context during the close of the Council

At the close of the Second Vatican Council seven messages were proclaimed to different "categories" of people. The expressed purpose of the messages was to identify partners in dialog with the Church.[2] The message to youth spoke very specifically about how the Church desired to reform itself so as to more clearly articulate the Gospel to be received by this and future generations. As the message indicates, "For four years the Church has been working to rejuvenate her image in order to respond the better to the design of her Founder, the great Living One, the Christ who is eternally young."[3] Envisioning themselves as the lightbearers who will soon pass the torch to a new generation, the bishops go on to express both hope and concern for the challenges the youth will experience in the modern world. By shining a light on the context of the address it will provide a means by which to evaluate the torchbearers themselves and what may have been intended in this message to youth.

The preparations of the Second Vatican Council were highly consultative and dialogical. The bishops exercised and developed their capacity for the challenging art of consultation and dialog during the years of preparation leading up to the Council and its four periods of deliberation. In his opening address, John XXIII described a Church open to receiving wisdom, ready to "gain in spiritual riches" and "new sources of energy." He anticipated "timely changes" through "a prudent system of mutual cooperation."[4] Even before the Council's opening address, its leaders had made great effort to consult the universal Church, reading through thousands of *vota* (responses) from bishops and other individuals dispersed throughout the globe.

Yet the addresses that marked the conclusion of the Council would not necessarily reflect the same cooperation that John XXIII called for in his opening address or the "effort of getting to know" those they are addressing raised in Paul VI's encyclical, *Ecclesiam Suam*.[5] At the close of the Council on December 8, 1965, Pope Paul VI claimed the final messages were of the Council although they were "neither drafted nor approved by them."[6] While reflective of some of the essential developments of the Council Fathers' thinking, especially considering the deliberations in the final period on *The Pastoral Constitution of the Church in the World Today*, the addresses were developed with little consultation and likely no dialog with the youth whom the bishops addressed. Weariness from the four-year process and the two additional solemn sessions that preceded the closing liturgy on December 8 likely contributed to the manner in which the addresses were constructed.[7]

Despite this lack of consultation the bishops were keenly aware that the world was experiencing significant change. They wrote of such change in *Gaudium et Spes*: "Today, the human race is involved in a new stage of history. Profound and rapid changes are spreading by degrees around the whole world. . . . History itself speeds along on so rapid a course that an individual person can scarcely keep abreast of it."[8] Modern advances, such as the development of commercial air travel, enabled bishops to experience the first world ecumenical council, as evidenced by the sheer number of participants from all over the globe.[9] Events and developments such as the civil rights movement in the United States, the landing on the moon, the construction of the Berlin Wall, the growing independence of many African nations from their colonizers, and the growing threat of nuclear annihilation as evidenced in the Cuban Missile Crisis all contributed to the context in which the bishops gathered for the Second Vatican Council. The Church, aware of these realities and eager to engage the world in a new way, produced the decree *Gaudium et Spes* to address the issues of modernity when many modern cultures had already made or were in the process of transitioning to postmodernity.

In light of these cultural realities it seems significant to high-

light the youth as one of the seven categories of people for the bishops to reach out to in dialog. At the time there was no World Youth
Day, the first of which was held in Rome in 1986. Young adult ministry was not yet conceived, and in the United States a national association for young adult ministry, the National Catholic Young Adult
Ministry Association, was not formed until 1982 to support those
who minister to young adults in the Catholic Church. The bishops
of the United States published their first pastoral plan for ministry to
young adults in 1996. This address could therefore be seen as the
first major address from the Church to young people in postmodern
times—a first step toward an engaged and vibrant ministry to postmodern young adults. If the address to youth offered at the close of
the Second Vatican Council was intended as the beginning of a dialog with the youth, then young people have said quite a lot in reply
during these last forty-seven years.

The Council's address to youth

The message to youth is the last of the seven messages and
follows the pattern set in the previous six by affirming and calling
upon the intended audience, in this case "young men and women
of the world," to receive the message of Christ.[10] Yet in the message
to youth the Council adds, "It is for you, youth, especially for you
that the Church now comes through her council."[11] It seems that
the bishops intentionally place the message to youth as their final
address, recognizing that without the youth of the world the
renewed vision of Church developed in the Council may be lost in
the future. In his opening address regarding the Council, John the
XXIII explains, "What is needed is that this certain and immutable
doctrine, to which the faithful owe obedience, be studied afresh and
reformulated in contemporary terms. For this deposit of faith, or
truths which are contained in our time-honored teaching is one
thing; the manner in which these truths are set forth (with their
meaning preserved intact) is something else."[12] The Church,
through Council reform, is seeking to reframe its teaching to be
"more widely known, more deeply understood, and more penetrat-
ing in its effects on men's moral lives."[13] John XXIII calls for the
Council to aid the Church in its expression of the faith in a new way

so its treasures can be best received by the people of the day, and perhaps in particular received by the youth whose ongoing participation in the Church helps ensure the Church's continuation in the future. The approach taken by the Council is "in a manner more consistent with a predominantly pastoral view of the Church's teaching office" and "best served by explaining more fully the purport of her doctrines, rather than by publishing condemnations."[14]

Toward the end of his opening remarks during the closing liturgy of the Council Paul VI echoes John XXIII when he describes his hope for the reception of Vatican II in the world in the following way: "May it rise as a new spark of divine charity in our hearts, a spark which may enkindle the principles, doctrine and proposals which the council has organized and which, thus inflamed by charity, may really produce in the Church and in the world that renewal of thoughts, activities, conduct, moral force and hope and joy which was the very scope of the council."[15] This sense of Vatican II as a renewal of the consistent teaching of the Church is further commended in the message to youth when it claims, "For four years the Church has been working to rejuvenate her image in order to respond the better to the design of her Founder, the great Living One, the Christ who is eternally young. At the term of this imposing re-examination of life, she now turns to you."[16] It appears that the Council bishops seek the collaboration of youth such that the mission of the Church may be faithfully stewarded into the present realities of the world. Inferred in these statements is the argument that the *aggiornamento* and renewal found in Vatican II is not about making the Church more palatable for a new generation by watering down or changing Church teaching but rather about expressing the realities of a just and good God in ways that the modern world will be better able to hear and understand. The address appears to appoint the youth with a special role in communicating the teachings of the Church so the Gospel may be received by the modern world.

Having undergone the transformation brought about by the event of the Council, the authors of the address seem to express a Church closely associated with the youth and see the Church as rejuvenated by the reforms. As the commentator R. La Valle explains, "the Church...is called to a radical regeneration, in the measure in which the Greek *metanoia* and the Latin *reformatio* signify a new birth."[17]

The bishops sincerely hope that this newly reframed vision of the Church is not and will not be lost on the youth, and intentionally direct a message to youth to emphasize their importance. This message is cautionary about the world yet optimistic about what the youth will accomplish. The concern for society is not shared in a spirit of hope, as was the opening address of the Council, but out of anxiety.[18] The message sounds anxious that the young may continue to hold the faith of their elders despite the grasp that despair, annihilation, atheism, lassitude, egoism, and hedonism have on society. The address raises concerns about human dignity, religious liberty, and the rights of individuals that occupied the Council's discussions found in *Gaudium et Spes* and *Dignitatis Humanae*. Anxiety about the challenges of creating a better society grounded in human dignity is reflected in this message to the youth.

While these challenges are relevant and continue to be of great concern even today, the language of the address also seems to express optimism that the youth will persevere in modern society despite these difficulties. The address appeals to the energy and idealism of youth to confront the ills of society and to become a leaven in the world, communicating these core truths to all whom they encounter. This cautionary optimism provides a helpful lens in which to view the overall tone of the message to youth; it wants to celebrate the joy and the good that may be found and achieved in the world by young adults, but never loses sight of the real challenges they may encounter.

As a young adult seeking a sense of belonging in the faith community, it can be incredibly empowering and reassuring to hear, "It is for you, youth, especially for you that the Church now comes through her council to enkindle your light, the light which illuminates the future, your future."[19] The message suggests, "Be generous, pure, respectful and sincere, and build in enthusiasm a better world than your elders had."[20] While including reference to characteristics that resonate with young adults such as humility and justice, the message also acknowledges the way in which some have failed in the past with the hope that these same errors will not be repeated.[21] A young person reading and reflecting on this message might reasonably feel a sense of support and affirmation from the bishops that they can and will contribute to a better world.

The address concludes with two bold statements about the Church. It claims "the Church as the real youth of the world" and that young people will find in the Church "the genuine, humble, and wise Hero, the Prophet of truth and love, the Companion and Friend of youth." With the benefit of time and distance these claims will now be examined against the experience of young people today and propositions will be made on how the Church, taking inspiration from the Council, can more fully engage young adults today and in the future.

Engaging the youth of today

The young adults of the mid-sixties and those of today share many of the qualities of youth explored at the beginning of this chapter, but there are also differences. Even the term "young adult" is relatively new, and essentially refers to a new stage of development derived from a burgeoning of the middle-class where adulthood is delayed, self-identity is developed, and life pursuits are explored and determined. "Emerging adults," as termed by Christian Smith and Patricia Snell, describe those between the ages 18-29. Smith and Snell outline some of the reasons for this new life stage: (1) a dramatic growth in higher education in the United States due to the GI Bill, changes in the American economy, and the government subsidy of community college, (2) the delay of marriage, and (3) changes in employment that lead to lower job security, more frequent job changes, and ongoing training and education.[22] By contrast, in 1965 many in their early twenties did attend college and yet many more were still going directly from high school into the workforce,[23] women were only beginning to emerge in the office environment,[24] and people could expect to work for a company for years if not for their entire career, often with training for new skills or pathways for upward mobility within that same company. The life circumstances of the young adult today generally differ from those of their counterparts in the 1960's, and thus must be more fully explored to understand the ways in which they may receive and understand the address to youth which was written in a very different time period.

An examination of postmodernism as the context in which young people are formed provides a helpful lens through which the experiences and values of the young adults of today may be understood. Smith and Snell describe the general trends about this current generation of young adults and offer great nuance to their experience by identifying six different religious types of emerging adults (Committed Traditionalists, Selective Adherents, Spiritually Open, Religiously Indifferent, Religiously Disconnected, and Irreligious).[25] Before exploring Smith and Snell's research, it will be helpful to consider how the life circumstances of young adults are formed within a postmodern society. This contextualization will aid our analysis of the Second Vatican Council's address to youth and assist in extrapolating the ways this address is prophetic and where it is in need of reform.

Leonard Sweet describes the postmodern experience and how the Church needs to respond to this reality in order to gain the attention and attendance of young people. Postmodern culture, according to Sweet, is E.P.I.C.: Experiential, Participatory, Image-Driven, and Connected. He proposes that the Church needs to return to the practices of the early Christians, "more apostolic than patristic."[26] In other words, young adults would identify more closely with a Church that emphasizes community and mission than one that emphasizes propositions and orthodoxy, or "correct beliefs." Keeping this distinction in mind, we turn now to clarifying and describing what it means to say that young adults live in an E.P.I.C. world.

Youth today seek to enter fully, with their whole selves—body, mind, and spirit—into the experiences that life has to offer. They want to experience what life *is*, not what it is *about*.[27] Passive learning such as reading and lectures have migrated to more interactive learning such as applications found on most mobile devices and online learning communities. Steve Jobs and Apple, Inc., may provide a good example of this focus on experience; people line the streets for the opening of a new Apple store for the *experience* of being one of its first shoppers. Workshops are held right in the store and the employees and structure of the store are intended to highlight what the product can *do* through an *experience* of the feature, not through explanation. So, for example, you would not hear the salesperson describe the two-way videophone feature called Face Time. Instead, you can call the person on the iPad next to you and see their face, experiencing the application first hand. One learns about the feature by *experiencing* the feature. New consumers are continually wowed when they realize there is no waiting in line to check out. The sales team doubles as on-the-floor "geniuses," ready to respond to your product questions, swipe your credit card right where you are standing on their hand held iPhone and send you on your way with a receipt sent to your e-mail. Apple is deeply in tune with the postmodern desire to enter into an experience.

For the sake of comparison, consider your experience of the Catholic Church if you were to enter a dozen different churches for Sunday liturgy. What sort of experience might be offered? Ideally those who enter a church would be able to *experience* Church, not just hear about what it means to be a community of faith. How are beliefs such as the continuing self-communication of God's grace, justice, charity and community experienced within the context of the parish community? Thoughtful consideration of how young people are experiencing the Church is worthwhile.

Sweet goes on to define the culture of the postmodern young person as participatory. Postmodern culture shies away from a representative culture, where a few are delegated responsibility for the many. Instead, postmodern culture may be described as interdependent and fluid, a web of connections that diminishes traditional lines of authority and where each person becomes an expert by nature of the fact that they are a content provider with a unique experience. Young adults expect to interact with their surroundings. Consider the online forums with various wikis—websites that allow collaborative editing of its content and structures by all the users. As Sweet explains, "electronic culture pushes postmoderns towards more active and interactive behaviors."[28] Recently Bjork, the Icelandic pop musician, released a new album, *Biophilia*. The album comes with an application that allows the listener to participate in the song by touching the iPad screen. Every touch changes the speed or tone of the song so that the user becomes a co-creator of the music with Bjork. Not only does the user have a unique experience, but she or he also contributes his or her own uniqueness into the song—something that no other person can do at that moment. The song is now a unique creation between the composer and the user. *Biophilia's* song application is a perfect example of the participatory nature of postmodern young adults.

For the Church, addressing this need for young adults to contribute and feel valued for each of their unique gifts and talents can be significant. Young adults of a postmodern generation are not likely to want to be just another cog in a wheel but rather to make use of their interests and passions that contribute in a special way. Such participatory experience may lead to the full, conscious, and active participation called for in *Sacrosanctum Concilium*. Decades after the Council we are only beginning to uncover how to engage people in the celebration of the Eucharist. Sweets's observations about participation would seem to move us beyond the mere assignment of roles at the liturgy to preparing and encouraging the engagement of young people leading up to and flowing from the liturgy. Creative techniques and strategies that offer individual and group reflection of the Sunday scriptures would help young adults enter into full participation at the liturgy. Connecting service projects and everyday actions with the concluding rite at Mass might help young adults to see the connection of the Eucharist to our pursuit for a more just world.

The next characteristic of the postmodern culture Sweet describes is image-driven. He contrasts the highly metaphoric experience of postmodern culture with the rational propositional approach of modernism and reminds us that our inclination toward images and metaphor is not new. The sacramental imagination of our Church points to this reality. Yet in the modern age rational thought pushed our propensity toward images to the background. To reach this generation and future generations the Church, Sweet argues, we will need to tap into that deep well of metaphor and story that touches the heart. This generation will be far less inclined to respond to theological treatises or apologetics than they will be to modern day parables.

The preaching and outreach ministries of the Church, therefore, may need to reassess the prevailing needs of the day. The rich traditions and history of the Church need not be overlooked, but a

Church community whose catechesis never connects faith with the lived experience of its members will fail to capture the imaginations and hearts of its adherents. Art and architecture can be brought forward in our catechesis to help express our faith. Young adults, who are generally open and more inclusive of others, may be more likely to participate in a faith tradition that makes an effort to have a diversity of images that represent God and includes their experiences in the community of believers. How do we invite individuals to see God within their own lives and in the life of the community? How does the Church see the experiences of its members as informing the images it uses to preach the Gospel or in how it understands the Corporal Works of Mercy or other lived expressions of faith?

The final word that Sweet uses to describe the postmodern experience is connected. He illustrates this point with the equation Be=We/Me: "A postmodern 'me' needs 'we' to 'be.'"[29] This connectedness, however, is always the individual's choice. Today's postmodern young people choose who are their "friends" on Facebook, select "groups" on Google+, and join "networks" on LinkedIn. If the Church is to reach this population of young people we might seek to connect with them in various ways through various media (not all need to be digital) and recognize that young adults make connections by personal choice based on common interests, not out of some philosophical or ideological proposition. Young adults seem to hold their loyalty with groups that "check in" with them throughout the day and week. Parishes that can capitalize on this new way of communicating using social media with young adults would seem more likely to engage this generation.

Perhaps one of the Church's most appealing beliefs for a postmodern young adult's sense of "connectedness" is the belief in the communion of saints. Here the Church can take advantage of the vast network found in the cloud of witnesses of our tradition where we join together with all those who have gone before us and all who will follow after us in faith. And as most catechists know, "faith is not taught, it's caught." The Church needs strong catechesis or it cannot effectively preach its mission, but the best catechesis will be one that inspires deep relationships in which all people, young and old, have a shared sense of mission born from and lived out in community. Church leaders would be wise to understand, however, that a postmodern young adult belongs to a Christian community because it shares his or her values and beliefs, not simply because it is convenient or expected. Belonging is a choice that young adults make, not a requirement to be imposed.

In her assessment of young adults, *Big Questions, Worthy Dreams*, Sharon Daloz Parks rightly identifies the need to belong and the need to make a difference as the essential defining forces of young adulthood.[30] When communities meet these two needs, whether religious or otherwise, those communities will continue to engage young adults. For the Church, this means that it needs to help young adults feel as though they belong to the faith community and that their presence within it matters and makes a difference. Without this sense of belonging, or shared mission, too many young adults won't even be there to listen to any messages the Church may have to give them. While acknowledging that the message to youth was to all youth regardless of faith tradition, the message seems to speak more to the role of young adults in the world than what they may have to contribute to the faith community. To continue engaging young adults today the Church may need to seriously reflect upon how its own structures and activities hold up to the claims made in the address about the Church and the critique it makes of society.

In addition to the characteristics of young adults addressed above, the hearts and minds of emerging adults are shaped by some of the following themes, outlined by Smith and Snell: a multiplicity of transitions, moral subjectivity, standing on one's own, and being submerged in interpersonal relationships.[31] Due to job changes, the need to consistently learn new skills in order to remain competitive in the job market, changes in relationships in the home (moving back in with family, moving out, living with roommates, divorces, deaths, etc.), changes in relationships with friends and co-workers, changes in their dating and romantic relationships, emerging adults experience an almost overwhelming amount of transition. The significant number of new challenges and experiences one has during this period of life introduces an emerging adult to a great diversity of people and thinking. This diversity of perspective has led to a generation characterized by an open-mindedness that tends to believe that each person has a different and unique perspective which is uniquely his or her own and that shapes one's entire reality.

The deep immersion of the person in experience noted by Sweet and described in the research done by Smith and Snell means that this generation generally has "great difficulty grasping the idea that a reality that is objective to their own awareness or construction of it may exist that could have a significant bearing on their lives. They seem to presuppose that they are simply imprisoned in their own subjective selves, limited to their biased interpretations of their own sense perceptions, unable to know the real truth of anything beyond themselves."[32] While the idea of objective truth may not be understood, by and large they do believe that identifying right from wrong is easy and that "not hurting others is self-evident."[33] More often than not, emerging adults feel that if you "do good" you will be rewarded and that "morality is a personal, relative affair."[34]

The most important life task for this age group, as identified by Smith and Snell, is to learn how to "stand on one's own two feet."[35] They are moving from the dependence of living with their parents to independence and self-sufficiency. They feel overwhelmed by all the skills and life decisions they need to make, such as learning how to buy a car, interview for a job, negotiate properly for their salaries, learn about their health care options, learn new job cultures, and so on. While emerging adults know they can turn to their parents or other trusted mentors for advice, they frequently feel the pressure and understand the importance of being self-sufficient and able to stand on one's own without the need of assistance from anyone else. The economy has complicated this desire for self-sufficiency, however, and current research suggests that thirty-nine percent of emerging adults in the United States currently live or have recently lived with their parents due to many factors.[36] Of those that do live at home, seventy-eight percent indicate that they don't have enough money to live the life they want to live, a point that certainly aligns with Smith and Snell's data. Even though many emerging adults may not have made the full transition out of their parent's homes, they still feel that desire to be self-sufficient and stand on their own.

The personal growth and change that emerging adults constantly undergo does not necessarily mean that they are entirely self-absorbed and uninterested in being part of a community. The Corporation for National and Community Service maintains records related to volunteering in America, and the number of Millennials who volunteer has steadily increased from 6.1 million in 2003 to 11.6 million in 2010. As a group Millennials offered over 1.2 billion hours of community service in 2010, a significant contribution to others in society. While this demonstrates a growing awareness of the need to give back to one's community, Millennials still volunteer at a rate of 21.2 percent in contrast to the average national volunteer rate of 26.3 percent in 2010.[37] Smith and Snell's research concludes that emerging adults do not have the money necessary for the lifestyle they desire and are less likely to volunteer their time and make philanthropic contributions, a finding that would offer an explanation as to why Millennials volunteer at lower rates than other demographic groups. Instead of volunteering now, emerging adults anticipate making charitable contributions later in life when they have more money and time to give. As a general trend, emerging adults seem to feel that charity, whether of time or money, is the responsibility of those who have greater quantities of those resources than they do at this time.

Smith and Snell discovered that this generation has a strong desire for interpersonal relationships and will spend most of their time developing relationships and engaging with family and close friends. This is different than being active in organized groups. In fact, most emerging adults are not involved in clubs or extra-curricular activities but would prefer to spend time "hanging out" with those they know best. All of this, again, begs the question of how the Church might best respond to the attitudes and mindsets of young adults. While craving relationships, they are not necessarily "joiners" and perceive themselves as not having the time, financial security, or need to have a community beyond their friends and family. The Church must attempt to address the reality that, for many young adults, its ability to offer moral guidance is both unwanted and perceived as unnecessary. Instead, one of the primary ways it will maintain a connection with young adults is through the strength of interpersonal relationships. Without those personal connections, young adults may very well leave—and in many cases have already left—the faith community. Developing authentic relationships where the Church can respond to some of the real-life concerns of young adults identified by Smith and Snell can lead to further engagement of young people today.

Addressing the young people of today

Having explored the circumstances surrounding the initial address and an exploration of the postmodern culture and the general trends identified for young adults we turn now to exploring what the address to youth is able to say to young adults fifty years after the opening of the Second Vatican Council. An analysis of key parts of this very brief address follows, with attention given not only to how it is relevant to this generation of youth but also to uncovering what more would need to be said to properly address the needs of young adults today.

Firstly, by nature of the fact that the youth are one of the seven categories of people addressed by the Council, the address shows that there is great interest in and concern for young people. It is true that since this address there have been many efforts by the Church, both worldwide as well as in the United States, to address the needs and concerns of youth and coordinate ministerial efforts in a more cohesive way. From the development of the office of youth within the Pontifical Council for the Laity at the Vatican, to World Youth Day, to national organizations like the National Catholic Young Adult Ministry Association, to the many books, courses, and ministry programs specifically dedicated to serving this population, the Church has grown tremendously in its service and outreach to young people. These offices, ministries, and academic efforts mobilize vast amounts of resources worldwide to aid the pastoral response to young adults.

This pastoral outlook corresponds to the thoughtful reflection and impulse of the bishops to include the youth as one of the key audiences who had not yet been satisfactorily addressed in the writings of Vatican II. In the message, the Council claims a particular interest in the experiences and challenges of youth in the world, and such expressions of humility and authenticity are essential for connecting with young people. As Frank Mercadante explains, "because postmodern truth is based in practical reality, it is also related to their [young adults'] preference for authenticity. Instead of focusing on what one should be, and therefore, creating distance between one another, people should deal with their honest realities and open the door to experience greater connection and intimacy. Postmoderns are not looking for something to believe in as much as a community in which to belong."[38] The address to youth seems to show a desire by the leadership of the Church to develop a closer relationship to young people, but unless the youth have a personal relationship with the bishops offering the address it may not be seen as particularly relevant or noteworthy for them. For a young adult to feel intimately and authentically connected to the Church today, all pastoral leaders will need to build relationships that indicate a genuine interest in the experiences and contributions of young adults.

The leadership that any young adult may be able to offer in the Church will be done in a context that the Council Fathers presciently understood to be one of great change, "For it is you who...live in the world at the period of the most gigantic transformations ever realized in its history."[39] Although initially addressed to young adults in the midst of the industrialized transformation of the 1960's, the current generation of young people are living through a digital transformation that has vastly changed both the medium of communication and the ways in which people connect to one another. The young adults of today, as previously noted, live lives in which they are constantly undergoing transitions. Young adults who accept the torch of leadership that has been extended to them will be fully embracing the openness to change that the bishops themselves have identified as one of the most celebrated qualities of youth.

Although young adults have many qualities that will allow them to be effective leaders in the Church, that leadership will be challenged by the realities of the society in which they live. Intriguingly, the message to youth contains the optimistic hope that the youth will succeed in addressing these challenges where others have previously failed. "The Church...has confidence that you will find such strength and such joy that you will not be tempted, as were some of your elders, to yield to the seductions of egoistic or hedonistic philosophies or to those of despair and annihilation, and that in the face of atheism, a phenomenon of lassitude and old age, you will know how to affirm your faith in life and in what gives meaning to life, that is to say, the certitude of the existence of a just and good God."[40] Again, the bishops in the address express an optimistic hope that young adults will be able to address the ills of society and create a better world. While not explicitly indicated, one may also reasonably question how these assertions apply to the Church and whether there is anything in the bishops' message that might allow the youth to help shape the future of the Church in addition to their contributions to civil society.

Many of the concerns cited by the address are still important for today's emerging young adults. As discussed earlier, the efforts of emerging adults "getting on their own two feet" naturally drive them to focus on themselves for basic survival, often leading to egoistic or hedonistic choices. This stage of life brings most to focus on pursuits that strengthen them for greater contribution in the world later. Most do not expect to change the world, per se, but instead to make a difference with those who immediately surround them. Young adults generally feel that "helping others is an optional, personal choice." And their pursuit of pleasure can be characterized by their opinion of consumerism: Smith and Snell note the belief of young adults that "as long as people can afford their purchases, they are fully entitled to buy and consume whatever they want."[41] Atheism has also grown in the United States recently, and Smith and Snell note that the nonreligious nearly doubled between 1972 and 2006.[42] In addition, the hope the bishops had that Catholic young adults would know and affirm their faith also seems to be slipping in this generation; young adult attendance at Mass has significantly declined and young adult Catholics are less likely to identify as strongly religious than those of other Christian traditions.[43]

Although many of the concerns originally outlined by the bishops in the 1965 address to youth thus continue to be challenges today, this generation of young adults have confronted the bishops' concerns about "despair" and "annihilation" well. Generally speaking, young adults are optimistic about their future, despite any obstacles they may have already endured.[44] Furthermore, their core moral principle of not hurting others and their basic belief that "what goes around comes around" would likely divert the interests of most young adults from policies and global interventions that would cause great injury or harm.[45] Thus, the optimism for young adult leadership is not completely misplaced, as the very tendency that can sometimes lead older generations to classify young adults as naïve and idealistic provides them with the much needed determination and eschatological vision to believe that life can and should be more than what it is.

The address demonstrates the bishops' prioritization of young people, it acknowledges the significant transformations of society that young adults are experiencing, and it describes the humility and authenticity possible and experienced by the Church fathers through the Second Vatican Council. Yet the last paragraph is a bold statement made on the Church's behalf and one that could be critiqued in light of its ministry to young adults in the past few decades: the address describes the Church as "the real youth of the world," having the "strength and the charm of youth," able to give itself "unreservedly" and to "renew" itself. It would be fair, given what has been described above about young adult's participation in the Catholic Church, to suggest that the Church has more to do in order to realize such claims. In light of what is known about the young adults of today and our postmodern context the following efforts could bring the Church closer to the claims made in the address to youth: (1) The Church must respond pastorally to the need of young adults; (2) The Church must engage all young people to participate in the Church, regardless of their level of faith or commitment; (3) The Church must fully celebrate the Sacraments so as to ignite the sacramental imagination of young people; and (4) The Church must help young people to belong, and challenge them to grow spiritually.

Pastoral response to young people

The original insight for undertaking the Second Vatican Council was to reshape the Church's pastoral approaches so that its message might be received more fully by the people of the world.

This posture of dialog that begins with the mode of the receiver is instructive; it takes the concerns, struggles, joys, and hopes of the person, and the Church responds in a way that encourages growth toward Christ. This is not a new approach and, in fact, explicitly fits with our understanding of God and the economy of salvation; God first gifts us, loves us, and saves us, and it is only then that we can respond. Similarly, the Church cannot ask for the involvement and participation of young adults when, in most cases, those same young adults can respond, "What have you done for me lately!" This may sound like the egoism that the bishops warned about in the address, but we know that this response is theologically correct. If the Church is not living the Gospel message so that young people can see and understand it in their own lives, in light of their own struggles, challenges, and fears, then why would these young adults respond to and identify with the Church?

As indicated earlier, the Church needs to become more apostolic and, as Mercadante explains, the Church needs to "Immanuelize," to be "God with us" in the life and world of young people as a way to evangelize.[46] Albert Winseman, the Gallup Organization's Global Practice Leader for Faith-Based Organizations, lists knowing "What do I get?" as the initial stage of what he calls the Engagement Pyramid based on his organization's research.[47] Knowing the person and responding to the pastoral needs of the person is an essential starting place where the Gospel message may take hold. The Church would do well to focus less on programs and more on people.

An emphasis on people will help build a connected community that engages people in a participatory, image-driven experience. Each person has a story, and it is essential that the community of faith knows those stories and is able to celebrate, challenge, and mourn with the individuals that make up the community. Allow us to share a story from Peter's life that will demonstrate the very real way in which it is the people, not the programs, which help individuals to feel as though they belong:

> When I was in my early teenage years, I stopped going to Church. I began to get involved in the Church in high school again because of my friends. But I stayed because

of the community. It was true to say that I felt "known" by the parish community. Adults at the Mass I attended would spend upward of an hour after Mass speaking with me. These adults drove me to and from different ministry events. One even taught me how to drive a car and helped me get my driver's permit. Another taught me how to tie a tie for graduation (my father passed suddenly when I was a junior in high school, before I learned such things). Another parishioner gave me a summer job. Another taught me how to balance my checkbook. I would vacation with friends and family members that I met at Church. And when I could not afford college, parishioners helped me by paying the balance of my tuition that I did not receive through grants and loans. I was the only one of four boys to graduate from college, due in large part to the generosity of the incredible faith community to which I belonged.

The Church was never simply a place or series of programs or events for me in my adolescence as it was for me growing up as a child. The Church from my teenage years on has always been the people. And most important, they were people who knew my hopes, dreams, challenges and struggles. When my father passed away in the Spring of my junior year in high school, I had never experienced such an outpouring of love and care as that which I received from the people of my Church. I am convinced as I look back at that time that I chose my faith and future path in ministry because the actions of that Catholic community lived the Gospel message that I heard when I attended Mass on Sunday. The Catholic Church knew me, loved me, and I responded.

To truly respond to the needs of young adults requires that the community takes an interest in them on a personal level, gets to know their hopes and dreams, and invites them into an authentic relationship that helps them to feel as though they belong. When this happens, the Church no longer becomes an institution with which individuals have only a very loose affiliation if any, but a community of believers who care for one another and whose lives are intertwined in a holy way.

Engage all young people to participate in the Church, regardless of their level of faith or commitment

The faith community can no longer afford to assume that young adults who aren't currently present will return at some point in the future, perhaps to be married or to baptize their first child. Neither can it assume that those that are gone are forever lost and that any outreach is a wasted effort. The Gospel story of the shepherd leaving the ninety-nine in search of the one who is lost comes to mind, in part because of the radical, reckless love of God that is displayed. While engaging young people to participate in the Church will take a certain amount of time and energy, doing so is essential for the ongoing relevance of the Church in the world today. Creating and sustaining outreach efforts to young adults (and to others who are missing from the faith community) certainly helps to ensure that the Church will continue to have members past the current generation, but also, more importantly, serves as a faithful witness and response to God's love. We should engage young adults not only because they have something unique to offer the Church—although that is true—but also because God has loved us and we should share that love with others.

Engaging young adults in the faith community might begin with lay and clerical leaders intentionally inviting and listening to the needs of young adults. As has been already noted, if the address to youth were drafted today it might include greater consultation with the young adults themselves in the drafting of the document. All of the addresses from the close of the Council are clearly and intentionally meant as statements *from* the bishops *to* the various groups of people. Since the Council, greater attention has been paid to listening to the needs and experiences of those for whom the documents have been written, and these documents have often expressed a spirit of partnership with the various constituencies. For example, the development of the U.S. statement on young adults from the national bishops' conference, *Sons and Daughters of the Light*, was crafted with the assistance of young adults. At World Youth Day 2011 in Spain, Pope Benedict XVI spoke to the youth gathered and encouraged them to participate in the life of the Church and to share their experience of Christ with others.[48] The Pope's address is slightly more specific about the participation of the youth than the address to youth at the end of the Second Vatican Council, in which young people were mostly cautioned about the ills of the world and asked to hold to their faith. In the 2011 World Youth Day address there is a greater sense of the youth participating in the ongoing work of the Church as engaged partners.

This willingness to engage young adults as partners helps to counteract the way many young adults experience their lives within the faith community. Perhaps more than any other group, young adults are "betwixt and between," existing in a liminal space in which they are no longer children to be catechized but are also not quite yet members of the parish in the same way as older adults.[49] In a study published by the Center for Research in the Apostalate (CARA) in 2000, 54 percent of young adults indicated they would be more likely to participate in parish life if they felt welcome in the parish, 48 percent if there were opportunities to help the poor and needy, and 35 percent if there were quality worship.[50] When compared with other generational groups, young adults consistently ranked each of these as more important than any other group.

Offering authentic leadership opportunities to young adults within the structure of parish life would be one way of ensuring that they feel welcome and would help develop that ongoing sense of connection to the faith community beyond simply showing up on Sunday to pray with other Catholics. And while what qualifies as quality worship may differ greatly among individuals, generally speaking this refers to worship that engages the hearts and minds of active participants, a sentiment supported by Vatican II documents and that would seem to be supported by many Catholics, young adults or not. The issue of justice and outreach is one that will be explored in more depth later on, but it is significant to note that in the CARA report referenced above, all generations surveyed consistently ranked helping others as a key indicator of Catholic faith. For young adults, however, the parish community has a particular role to play in providing those volunteer outreach opportunities for parishioners since, unlike many of the other generational groups, young adults see providing ways to serve the poor and needy as one of the most important things the Church provides. As young adults ask the question "What do I get?" as it relates to their membership in the parish community, creating and sustaining volunteer outreach efforts, vibrant worship, and membership in an authentic community are some of the key ways the Church can respond and engage young adults.

The second step in Winseman's Engagement Pyramid is the response to the question, "What do I give?"[51] As discussed earlier, this generation, perhaps more than any previous, is seeking to *participate* as a way of *experiencing* life. This may and probably should cause us to rethink some of the very essentials of our ministry with young adults. Young people will not be satisfied solely with lectures or guest speakers. Homilies may need to be retooled to properly engage the receiver and acknowledge the multiplicity of experiences within the assembly. Have we thoroughly explored what it means to be fully active and participating in the liturgy? Additionally, young adults come with all sorts of skill that the Church desperately needs: information technology, business administration, accounting, civil law, construction, landscaping, interior design, plumbing, community organizing, teaching, advertising, musical theory and performance, child development, secretarial work, project management; the list goes on and on. There is no shortage of need in today's parish for skills like these, many of which young adults have learned and have already exercised within their campus ministry setting at colleges and universities.

Thankfully, today there are projects dedicated specifically to assisting young adults with their re-entry into the parish community after college, one of which is ESTEEM, Engaging Students to Enliven the Ecclesial Mission. A joint project of the National Leadership Roundtable on Church Management and the St. Thomas More Catholic Chapel and Center at Yale University, ESTEEM currently works with eight university campus ministries around the United States to prepare young adults for volunteer leadership positions on pastoral and finance councils, and in some cases for paid leadership positions, in parishes and dioceses. The Church could use more efforts like this one to encourage and train young adults to be good and faithful stewards when they return to parish life.

Individual parishes will need to find the right fit for each young adult and to consider how young adults might contribute in meaningful ways to the parish community and within its various ministries. John Roberto, a master practitioner in faith formation with an entrepreneurial spirit, suggests that parishes use scenario planning to reach out and respond to the various young adult religious types suggested in Smith and Snell's work.[52] The proper discernment of gifts and needs is one that is relevant not just for young adults but for the entire faith community. It is a failure on the part of the Church to relegate young adults solely to running the youth ministry or teaching religious education without attention to whether the charism of working with children is one that an individual possesses. The Church as a whole needs to call forth the gifts of each of its members in more dynamic ways. It is the entire faith community that suffers when only one type of person is seen as being able to contribute to a particular aspect of that community.

All of this speaks to the need of all church ministries to reflect the diversity of the community that gathers to pray together. This attention to diversity helps because it can keep the community from developing silos in which only certain members are welcome, and it also allows members to feel as though they may authentically contribute in more than one way. The gifts and generosity of all members may be fully welcomed and appreciated in a community in which openness, transparency, and genuine invitation and hospitality are present (qualities celebrated by many young adults). When the bishops implore young adults to faithfully respond to the needs of the world, they must be given the ability to do so at the parish and diocesan levels, not only within civil society. An excerpt from the address to youth describes the mission of young adults that could offer a major impact on the life of the world, but also on that of the Church. Young adults are "to open your hearts to the dimensions of the world, to heed the appeal of your brothers, to place your youthful energies at their service. Fight against all egoism. Refuse to give free course to the instincts of violence and hatred which beget wars and all their train of miseries."[53] The qualities and characteristics outlined in the address are ones that speak to that sense of inclusive love evident at the beginning of Paul VI's closing address of the Council, and which will allow a more credible interaction with both skeptics and people of good will.

Young adults, those who are and will create the future of the Church, must be attentive to how the Church remains relevant in the world today. In keeping with the vision and language of the Council, one must consider that the way in which the Church presents itself affects the way in which the Church's message may be heard. The Church need not be silent and should always continue its ministry of evangelization, but its message will be more thoughtfully considered if it is seen as a message of invitation rather than one of condemnation. Young adults have an important role to play in communicating the beliefs of the Church in the world today, and they must be able and invited to do so in creative ways that make use of technology, social media, and the cultural expressions of contemporary society.

The newest gimmick is not always needed or even the best way of proclaiming the Gospel, but the Church does need to think seriously about how it communicates its message in a manner that may be most easily heard and understood. This also requires serious consideration of how to address the critiques that many people, both Catholics and non-Catholics, may make of the Church. Many, but not all, young adults will question whether the Church really means what it says about its inclusive love for all of humanity when many of its members struggle to care compassionately for and welcome homosexuals, for instance. When the Church fails to speak out on behalf of non-Catholics who are being unfairly treated, such as when an Islamic high school applying for membership in a private association is asked to provide explanation beyond that of another similar institution simply because it is run by Muslims, the Church fails to honor its proclamations of human dignity, justice, and religious freedom. And when it fails to properly discipline its lay and ordained ministers who break the trust of the communities they serve through actions of fraud, embezzlement, and most abhorrently, the sexual abuse of children, the Church unequivocally fails to model the self-emptying love of Jesus in the world today. Those who share these concerns are by no means limited exclusively to young adults, but because of the young adult desire for authentic communities, any hypocrisy or failure on the part of the Church to clearly live out its core values will lead to the exodus of many young adults from the community.

The Church cannot afford to ignore its responsibility to speak the truth of God in the world today. Like the best of what the Church considers to be the qualities of youth, the Church must be open to change, continually renewing itself, seeking new challenges and opportunities, and committing wholeheartedly to each of these actions. When the Church does this, it will truly become a Church that inspires and engages youth and young adults who want and will be able to feel as though they truly belong and that they can make a difference not just within the faith community but in the entire world.

Ignite the sacramental imagination of young people

One of the ways that we can engage young people and have greater participation in the life of the faith community is by tapping into their image-driven tendencies through a fuller celebration of the Sacraments and a more intentional use of sacramentals. We know through the work of Sweet that postmodern young adults are seeking the mystery already present in our rituals and rites of the Church. Yet in our efforts to celebrate the sacraments the Church must be careful not to rid our rituals of the *focal practices* that are essential to the full celebration of the sacraments themselves. Theologian Richard Gaillardetz explains focal practices as the "activities we undertake in order to obtain a desired good, but, and this is crucial, in some sense the goods we desire are internal to the practice—they cannot be separated. These practices, while often pedestrian, generally demand the cultivation of some basic discipline or skill, a certain degree of attentiveness, and they can be judged by some accepted standard of excellence."[54] All too often priests and pastoral ministers can take shortcuts in the preparation for and celebration of the sacraments. In part these challenges persist because our priests and pastoral leaders are being asked to take on more ministry, which leaves less time to, for instance, properly prepare oneself spiritually or pastorally to visit the sick or prepare for a homily. Sometimes, subtle yet important elements of the rituals are excluded due to the pastoral limits of time. Leaving generous time for sacred silence for quiet contemplation and prayer between the first and second readings, the homily, and after the community receives the body and blood of Christ is a frequently overlooked element of our focal practice cut for the sake of expediency. In other cases such exclusions may be due to the lack of knowledge of the priest or pastoral leader celebrating the sacrament. Removing the baptismal waters from the holy water fonts during Lent and creating a countersign of the permanency of our baptism, or celebrating adult confirmations alongside the elect at the Easter Vigil, disregarding the significance of the sacrament of baptism in both the elect and the candidates for full communion, are recent experiences and examples that come to mind. Yet, when sacraments are properly celebrated in their fullness and the ministers and the assembly are properly prepared, rarely, if ever, in our experience, does someone say that they wished the celebration of the sacrament took less time or that certain elements would be removed from the rite because of the length of the ritual.

Engaging the sacramental imagination of young adults will help them connect to the sacramental life of the faith community. Pastoral leaders could encourage young adults to identify the presence of God in the activities and experiences of everyday life. As a society and people change and develop, new images and expressions of divine revelation will occur. Providing a forum for such expression, using new technologies, addressing the issues of the day, celebrating our traditions while responding to new opportunities; all of these are ways of acknowledging that the Church is not a static monolith of an institution but a dynamic community of believers.

In keeping with some of the claims of the address to youth, young adults are likely to believe that part of the role of the Church is to model to the rest of the world what its most deeply held values are; in other words, the Church should demonstrate to others a sacramental worldview in which all of creation is imbued with God's grace and that each person, as someone created in the image and likeness of God, has inherent dignity and worth. In helping to develop a world in which the rights and dignity of all are respected, young adults will want to see a faith community that values the participation of all of its members. This means the lectors, extraordinary ministers of holy communion, ushers, catechetical teachers, parish and finance council members, and staff of the parish—in essence, the Church—help to represent the diversity of the community in relationship to race, ethnicity, gender, socio-economics, physical and mental ability, and generation. As parishes become more and more diverse, with multiple languages and cultures represented, the ideal community is one that celebrates the richness of its diversity in a manner that doesn't create two or three parallel communities but instead integrates its various members into one community. There may be a need or desire for Masses or catechesis in several languages, but the goal should always be to seek the experience of unity in diversity found in the triune God.

This attention to diversity will also lead to an invitation for all members to participate in the ministries of the parish, assuming they have received the proper training and preparation particular to those roles. At the eucharistic table we gather as the Body of Christ, a People of God rich in diversity which faithfully calls out the gifts of all its members and invites them to serve one another. When we are sent forth to continue bringing Christ to the world at the end of the eucharistic liturgy, the faith community should have different ministries and opportunities to support, encourage, and sustain us in living our faith in the world. This attention to diversity can help young adults feel as though they are able to assume various ministries and roles in the parish, but it will also provide real examples of how the Church values all of its members and models openness, respect for human dignity, and the values of equality and justice.

Living out a sacramental worldview, the Church will also display respect by being attentive to how it collaborates with non-Catholics and respectfully proclaims its message. The tone of humility found in the address to youth is one that many young adults would like to see carried over into the way the Church continues to evangelize. Some of the most deeply held values for young adults include listening, compassion, and openness. Practically speaking, this means that the Church that lives out these qualities and that addresses many of the concerns of young adults would value dialog over debate, empathy over exclusion, transparency over secrecy, and accountability over saving face. The Church that employs these characteristics wouldn't necessarily have to change its beliefs, but it would have to change the way in which it articulates them. Recent examples of the Church doing just this include the creation and ongoing work of ecumenical working groups, the Archbishop of Dublin tearfully apologizing for the heinous rape of children by priests, and the adoption of the Catholic Standards of Excellence®[55] by many dioceses, parishes, and Catholic organizations to ensure best practices in the fields of finance and human resources in the Catholic Church. Each of these actions demonstrating the willingness of members of the Church to engage in self-reflection allows the Church's message to be more easily heard by those outside the Church, and will therefore give the Church and its members more equity to transform the world in the manner outlined by the bishops in their message to youth.

To engage young adults interested in an authentic community of believers, the Church in its own ministries and parish life has to value and encourage its members to share their joys and hopes, griefs, and anxieties with one another.[56] There must be a sense of hospitality that welcomes all into the community of faith, and there also has to be a value placed on truly listening to the experience of others. While we cannot explore in depth the full range of current issues that concern young adults, a cursory look at some of the major societal influences will help situate how young adults may and may not experience the Church as that community of support that truly listens to all of their experiences. When 63 percent of young adults believe that homosexuality should be accepted by society[57] and over half know someone who is gay,[58] to maintain credibility with young adults the Church may need to pay more attention to the experience of gays and lesbians who feel isolated and excluded from the faith community. Realistically, many young adults have engaged in sexual relationships outside of the bonds of matrimony, and even within a marriage will rarely hesitate to use contraceptives, making the Church's pastoral response to their sexual behaviors important for young adults.[59] There are no easy answers as to how the Church pastorally responds to the experience of individuals while also faithfully proclaiming the beliefs and traditions of the Church, but the failure to address these issues openly and sensitively has been one reason that many young adults feel as though they have been excluded from the Church.

Most young adults who have made choices contrary to official Church teaching aren't necessarily hoping that the teaching will be changed but rather that they will no longer feel excluded from the community because of choices they have made. A student Sarah works with recently shared with her how members of this student's Catholic faith community ostracized her when she got pregnant and had the child without marrying the child's father. Rather than commending her for choosing life, they instead chose to question whether the child could authentically be baptized and whether she, as an unwed mother, should be able to receive the Eucharist. While certainly not the expected and accepted Catholic response to a situation of this sort, her real pain and the wounds caused by a community to which she had belonged and in which she had participated for twenty years has led to her separation from a Church, which, as she says, fails to practice the compassionate love of the Christ who comes to heal and welcome sinners. The deep and painful wounds that we inflict on one another as members of the Catholic community are among our greatest tragedies and one of the clearest reasons why some young adults have left the Church and no longer see it as a sacramental sign of God's presence in the world.

Helping them belong and challenging them to grow spiritually

The final two stages on Winseman's Engagement Pyramid are to help people belong to the parish and to help them to grow.[60] Even the marginally-engaged young adult (characterized as Selective Adherents in Smith and Snell's study and representing approximately 25 percent of the young adults) could benefit from learning what it means to be a member of a parish community. Key touchstones with young adults in the life of the parish, such as the sacraments of baptism and marriage, inquiry for full communion through the rite of Christian initiation of adults, and parish registration, would help young adults to explore the value and benefits of being a member of a parish community and include clear expectations on what it means to be a member of the community.

Once young adults know what is expected of them, how does the Church hold them accountable to their spiritual growth? Sometimes the Church wants to hold young adults accountable without the young adult first knowing what is expected of their participation. Lest it not be clear, spiritual growth is at the top of the pyramid of engagement and thus presupposes that the Church is responding to the needs of the young adult, that the young adults are participating, and that they have a sense of belonging in the Church. However, the opposite can be true as well. We can have young adults trying to be engaged in the parish but pastoral leaders may not challenge them enough or help them to grow spiritually, instead leaving them to undergo ongoing faith formation alone. This can lead to the young person becoming stagnant in their faith and eventually drifting away from the parish community. The final recommendation relies heavily on the first recommendation— the Church needs to respond to and know the young adults it hopes to engage.

Conclusion

It is clear that the experience of the Second Vatican Council shaped the development of the address to youth by pointing to the reform experienced through the Council and the specific societal issues raised in the address. While it was directed to the youth of a different generation, some of its themes remain relevant for today. Yet the claim that the Church is "the real youth of the world" can be challenged as we look at the last few decades of ministry to young people. Through greater attention to pastoral needs of young adults, more encouragement of meaningful participation, reaching them through a fuller expression of the sacramental imagination found within the rituals of our Church, helping them understand what is expected of them, and helping them grow spiritually through mutual accountability, young adults may yet be capable of looking upon the Church and finding "the face of Christ, the genuine, humble, and wise Hero, the Prophet of truth and love, the Companion and Friend of youth" described in the closing lines of the address to youth. Young adults crave authenticity and the assurance that we will "be doers of the Word and not merely hearers" (Jas 1:22). In a digital age in which information is literally at our fingertips and Googling potential significant others, employers, medical treatments and worthwhile charities has become the standard medium of discovery and exploration, the person or institution that fails to accurately represent itself will be immediately distrusted. The Second Vatican Council was a pastoral council, focused on the ways the Church seeks to communicate the Gospel. While the address to youth at the close of the Council was from the bishops to the youth, the youth of today seem to be addressing the Church and asking for her to double down on this pastoral outreach in a spirit of authenticity and truly listening to the experiences of all those who belong to the People of God. The Church, capable of mirroring the paradigmatic example of the Great Pastor, certainly has this capacity, and young adults naturally gravitate to those parishes where this outreach and example can currently be found.

Sarah L. Heiman, M.Div., *serves as a Program Associate at Mercy Center in Madison, CT, and is a former campus minister and adjunct instructor of theology at Sacred Heart University.* **Peter Denio** *is the Catholic Standards for Excellence Coordinator at the National Leadership Roundtable on Church Management and Faith Formation Coordinator at Ss. Peter and Paul Parish in Hoboken, NJ.*

DISCUSSION QUESTIONS

1. What is your experience with young adults in ministry? How might they be engaged?
2. The authors suggest that postmodern culture significantly impacts the way in which young adults are able to connect with institutions like the Catholic Church. Do you agree or disagree? How do you think culture impacts the message of the Church?
3. How have new technologies and societal changes offered new opportunities and challenges for the Church's message to be heard in the world today? Are there new ways of expressing Catholic belief that would allow it to be more easily heard and understood?

SUGGESTED READINGS

Sharon Daloz Parks. *Big Questions, Worthy Dreams: Mentoring Young Adults in Their Search for Meaning, Purpose, and Faith*. San Francisco, CA: Jossey-Bass, 2000.
Christian Smith and Patricia Snell. *Soul Searching: The Religious and Spiritual Lives of Emerging Young Adults*. New York: Oxford University Press, 2009.
Leonard I. Sweet. *Postmodern Pilgrims: First Century Passion for the 21st Century World*. Nashville: Broadman & Holman, 2000.
United States Conference of Catholic Bishops. *Sons and Daughters of the Light: A Pastoral Plan for Ministry with Young Adults*. Washington, DC: United States Catholic Conference, 1996.

NOTES

1. Address to Youth.

2. Giuseppe Alberigo, "The Conclusion of the Council and the Initial Reception," in *History of Vatican II: The Council and the Transition The Fourth Period and the End of the Council, September 1965—December 1965*, ed. Giuseppe Alberigo, English version edited by Joseph A. Komonchak (Maryknoll, New York: Orbis Books, 2006), 552.

3. Address to Youth, 2.

4. Opening Address, John XXIII, Second Vatican Council.

5. *Ecclesiam Suam*. Pope Paul VI (45).

6. Alberigo, "The Conclusion," 552.

7. Norman Tanner, *The Church and the World: Gaudium et Spes, Inter Mirifica* (Mahwah NJ: Paulist Press, 2005), 36.

8. *Gaudium et Spes* 4-5.

9. 2860 bishops attended the Second Vatican Council, nearly two times the amount at the First Vatican Council where approximately 1050 bishops attended a little less than 100 years before.

10. Address to Youth, 1.

11. Address to Youth.

12. Opening Address of Vatican II.

13. Opening Address of Vatican II.

14. Opening Address of Vatican II.

15. Closing Speech.

16. Address to Youth, 2.

17. Albergio, "The Conclusion," 568.

18. Opening Address of VII: "We feel that We must disagree with these prophets of doom, who are always forecasting worse disasters, as though the end of the world were at hand....We must recognize here the hand of God, who, as the years roll by, is ever directing men's efforts, whether they realize it or not, towards the fulfillment of the inscrutable designs of His providence, wisely arranging everything, even adverse human fortune, for the Church's good."

19. Address to Youth, 2.

20. Address to Youth, 3.

21. Mary E. Bendyna, and Paul M. Perl, *Young Adult Catholics in the Context of Other Catholic Generations: Living with Diversity, Seeking Service, Waiting to be Welcomed*, Working Paper 1 (Washington, D.C.: Center for Applied Research in the Apostolate, 2000).

22. Christian Smith and Patricia Snell, *Soul Searching: The Religious and Spiritual Lives of Emerging Young Adults* (New York: Oxford University Press, 2009), 5.

23. Thomas Brock, "Young Adults and Higher Education: Barriers and Breakthroughs to Success," *Transition to Adulthood* 20:1 (Spring 2010): "Before 1965, American colleges and universities were rarefied places populated mostly by white males from middle- or upper-income families." http://futureofchildren.org/publications/journals/article/index.xml?journalid=72&articleid=523&sectionid=3589.

24. "Why Do Women Outnumber Men in College?", The National Bureau of Economic Research. http://www.nber.org/digest/jan07/w12139.html "In 1960, the labor force participation of female college graduates in their twenties and thirties was low: only 39 percent of 30-to-34-year olds were employed and 47 percent of those employed were teachers; 73 percent had children at home."

25. Smith and Snell, *Soul Searching*, 166-68.

26. Leonard Sweet, *Postmodern Pilgrims: First Century Passion for the 21st Century World* (Nashville: Broadman & Holman, 2000), 28.

27. Sweet, *Postmodern Pilgrims*, 33.

28. Sweet, *Postmodern Pilgrims*, 56.

29. Sweet, *Postmodern Pilgrims*, 117.

30. Sharon Daloz Parks, *Big Questions, Worthy Dreams: Mentoring Young Adults in Their Search for Meaning, Purpose, and Faith* (San Francisco, CA: Jossey-Bass, 2000).

31. Smith and Snell, *Soul Searching*, 34-74.

32. Smith and Snell, *Soul Searching*, 45.

33. Smith and Snell, *Soul Searching*, 47.

34. Smith and Snell, *Soul Searching*, 51.

35. Smith and Snell, *Soul Searching*, 34.

36. Kim Parker, *The Boomerang Generation: Feeling OK about Living with Mom and Dad. Social & Demographic Trends* (Washington, D.C.: Pew Research Center, 2012).

37. "Volunteering of Millennials (born 1982 and after)." Corporation for National and Community Service. Last updated August 9, 2011. http://www.volunteeringinamerica.gov/special/Millennials-(born-1982-or-after).

38. Frank Mercadante, *Engaging A New Generation: A Vision of Reaching Catholic Teens* (Huntington IN: Our Sunday Visitor, 2012), 10.

39. Address to Youth.

40. Address to Youth, 2.

41. Smith and Snell, *Soul Searching*, 67-68.

42. Smith and Snell, *Soul Searching*, 101.

43. Smith and Snell, *Soul Searching*, 100-101.

44. Smith and Snell, *Soul Searching*, 36-37.

45. Smith and Snell, *Soul Searching*, 47-48.

46. Mercadante, *Engaging a New Generation*, 52.

47. Albert L. Winseman, *Growing an Engaged Church: How to Stop Doing Church and Start Being Church Again* (New York: Gallup Press, 2007), 83.

48. Pope Benedict XVI. Homily Final Mass, World Youth Day. Sunday 21, August 2011 Madrid, Spain.

49. Victor Witter Turner, *The Ritual Process: Structure and Anti-Structure* (Ithaca, NY: Cornell University Press, 1969).

50. Bendyna and Perl, *Young Adult Catholics*.

51. Winseman, *Growing an Engaged Church*, 87.

52. John Roberto., *Faith Formation 2020: Designing the Future of Faith Formation*. Lifelong Faith Associates & Vibrant Faith Ministries, 2010.

53. Address to Youth, 3.

54. Richard R. Gaillardetz, *Transforming Our Days: Spirituality, Community and Liturgy in a Technological Culture* (New York: Crossroad, 2000), 23.

55. The Catholic Standards for Excellence is a project of the National Leadership Roundtable on Church Management. www.CatholicStandardsForExcellence.org.

56. *Gaudium et Spes.*

57. Pew Forum on Religion & Public Life. *Religion Among the Millennials.* A Pew Forum on Religion & Public Life Report (Washington, DC: Pew Research Center, 2010).

58. Pew Research Center. *Millennials: Confident. Connected. Open to Change.* Millennials Generation Next Report (Washington, DC: Pew Research Center, 2010).

59. Lawrence B. Finer, "Trends in Premarital Sex in the United States, 1954-2003." *Public Health Reports* (The Guttmacher Institute, 2007):73-78.

60. Winseman, *Growing an Engaged Church*, 83.

To Workers

Work and the Working Life
Fifty Years after the Council

Nancy Dallavalle

Work is the defining feature of adult life. How we work, for whom we work, where we work and what we do there—all of this is bound up with our sense of ourselves as people engaged in an economy, in a public order, in families and, most intimately, in our own sense of ourselves as purposeful human beings. The very presence of detailed rubrics governing the dynamism of work and rest tells us that these two have always been problematically intertwined, so much so that to distill reflections on human "work" from reflections on human "life" is very difficult.

That this discussion will broaden the notion of "work" beyond paid employment is already clear, though compensation is, of course, an important social marker of how we regard our working selves. A young person in the United States today has often been at work as a student, member of a family, scout, choir member or teammate for years before receiving that first check at the age of seventeen for babysitting or washing dishes at a diner. Nevertheless, that check re-casts the activity of work, as it will again, perhaps for the same young person in his late twenties, now a college graduate (and bank clerk by day), who gets a first check from a magazine—all of $25.00, perhaps—for a poem he has crafted, bit by bit, over three months. Why is this? Why is the modest check in the mail in payment for the poem infinitely more valuable than his regular salary from the bank job? Obviously, the external confirmation of his talent as a poet matters more because the work of writing poetry is self-expressive in a way that the work of assisting with lost debit cards and opening savings accounts is not. Work, then, involves compensation, but it has a much broader anthropological function.

For many, however, this talk of work as purposeful or self-expressive is irrelevant, if not insulting. The work experience of the high school student who washes dishes or whacks weeds as a summer job before college is not the same as the experience of the forty-year-old immigrant to the United States who does the same work, year after year, struggling to make his paycheck and feed a family. Nor is this the same experience as that of the fifty-year-old woman, laid off from her job as a bookkeeper in a pleasant office, who now runs a register at a big box store, her restroom breaks carefully timed and her cash drawer checked by a manager before she clocks out. Though perhaps equally rewarding, the experience of working as a high-school math teacher is different at a public school in inner-city Baltimore than it is at a private prep school in rural Connecticut. Such disparities have always characterized the world of work, and they are certainly operative today, such that even a common label like "stay-at-home mother" covers a wide variety of experiences, expectations and burdens.

Nevertheless, cultural comparisons between the situation in the United States in 2012 and that in the 1960's also indicate some changing contexts for the discussion of work. As the Second Vatican Council closed in 1965, the United States had just begun to send troops to Vietnam, the 1964 Civil Rights Act by was being implemented by the 1965 Voting Rights Act, and President Lyndon Johnson signed what was generally regarded as a very modest, low-impact bill focused on united families, the 1965 Immigration and Naturalization Act.[1] These three examples, seemingly limited to particular issues, illustrate the cultural shifts that were happening in the United States (with numerous parallels in other industrialized nations), shifts that had immediate resonance for expectations about work. The war in Vietnam raised important questions about institutional authority and U.S. foreign policy, questions that came into the mainstream in a pointed way because the compulsory draft of young men for military service cut across the social fabric. The Civil Rights Act opened the door to expanded expectations for social enfranchisement, including programs that would bring a wide variety of formerly marginalized persons into the workforce. And immigration, of legal migrants as well as those without documentation, has profoundly shaped the workforce and, to some extent, the economy, in this country.

The intended—or unintended—ramifications of these policies indicate how broad a perspective is required to examine the notion of work, of working and of workers. While Pope John Paul II's great encyclical on work, *Laborem Exercens* (1981), most self-consciously stands in the line of Catholic social teaching since *Rerum Novarum*, the preface to the closing exhortation "To Workers," from the final session at Vatican II, situates its own concern for workers as the first fruit of the Pastoral Constitution on the Church in the Modern World, *Gaudium et Spes*. The closing exhortation is meant to indicate the breadth of the audience for the Second Vatican Council. That Council's explicit intention was to engage with the modern world and to receive that world in all its complexity. Yet any address of the working life is already also an address of the economic order ; indeed, the economic order has already shaped our imagination with regard to what "counts" as work and what does not. Thus "social justice" isn't something external that we decide to "apply" to an already given economic order. On the contrary, an implicit theory about social order—and a sense for what is just and what is not—is already operative in discussions of economic policy, however unacknowledged.[2] This essay will present an overview of the close connections between the discussion of work and the discussion of the social order in recent Catholic magisterial documents, and then turn to several issues— women, immigration, globalization and subsidiarity—that these connections keep in play, closing with a consideration of work as an example of co-operative grace.

Contextualizing work and workers

While sounding themes familiar to the contemporary Christian, a consideration of the historical context for the appearance of Leo XIII's *Rerum Novarum*, in1891, reminds us that these themes should not be taken for granted as givens for Catholic thought. Coming at a moment when Italy's working people were on the edge and certainly not favorably disposed toward the clergy, this text, putting forward a concern for the growing income and wealth gap, spoke in a manner that, while not adventurous theologically, was ready to break new ground in terms of its analysis of the concrete situation and its critique of the enfranchised. The document's intermittent tone of *noblesse oblige* should not obscure the genuine contribution of this text, in its basic call for a new approach in a time of change, and its specific advocacy for an economic and social order that recognizes fully the situation of workers and their dignity in the eyes of God (who, further, "lays down precepts yet more perfect, and tries to bind class to class in friendliness and good feeling," [RN 21]). Fully embracing both the notion of private property and the right of workers to organize [49], *Rerum Novarum* insists that the social order's most basic compact, between employers and the workers they hire, reflects some recognition of the full picture of the worker as a human person by the employer.

Ninety years later, John Paul II, a pope who had also spent time as a laborer, sets forward the notion that work has been "a constant factor both of social life and of the Church's teaching" in *Laborem Exercens*. While acknowledging the milestone of *Rerum Novarum*, the topic of work in itself, John Paul argues, is present from Genesis. Moreover, he argues the topic of work requires our attention due to "the fact that human work is a key, probably the essential key, to the whole social question, if we try to see that question really from the point of view of man's good."[3] Why is this? Because that "good" is never utilitarian, it is always realized in "the direction of 'making life more human,'"[3] and thus the Catholic approach to work, to workers, and to the working life must always be one that sees work as an exemplar for theological anthropology as this permeates the entirety of theology.

In particular, *Laborem Exercens* makes it clear that neither "labor" nor "capital" can be seen as merely material forces, to be plugged into an equation. On the contrary, the worker deserves a sense that "he is working *'for himself,'*" and therefore "*the principle of the priority of labour* over capital is a postulate of the order of social morality."[13] Thus it is with *Laborem Exercens* that the worker as an acting subject comes to the fore, not surprisingly, given the personalist anthropology of John Paul II. Yet Protestant theologian Miroslav Volf, reflecting on the text of *Laborem Exercens*, warns that such a subjective approach might deviate too far from the biblical notion of the human having dominion over the earth, such that "[d]*ominium terrae* is to be understood primarily as *dominium laboris.*"[3] Volf acknowledges, however, that the notion of the human having "dominion" over her or his own labor is simply an extension of the Catholic claim, in *Gaudium et Spes* [63], that the human person is "the source, the center, and the purpose of all economic and social life." While differing on the notion of dominion, Volf does find common cause with much of John Paul II's approach, recognizing, with the pontiff, that the real world economic systems of capitalism and communism do explicitly displace the human, and thus this anthropology remains an important perspective in a world in which, increasingly, "*things* rule over persons."[4]

Further employing an evangelical perspective, Volf also wonders if John Paul has adequately inquired about the purpose of work and the relationship between work and the satisfaction of needs, finding that the latter, for contemporary people, seems to be in the state of "a self-enforcing spiral without limit." (Volf writes in 1983; surely he would find even more evidence for concern about rising expectations today.) Biblically, Volf argues, there are limits to these needs, citing three in particular: concern for the earth, a concern to keep work on a human scale and, most importantly in scripture, a concern for the needs of the poor. Drawing on texts from the gospels and the Pauline corpus, Volf observes that social justice was part of the Christian perspective on work from the first: "The early Christians emphasized care for the needs of the underprivileged as one of the most important purposes of work. Working to satisfy the needs of others is possible only when one limits one's own needs." In other words, my own standard of living should be such that care for others is included in that "standard." Moreover, Volf claims, the need to care for others should, in itself, be a strong motivator for work (a move he does not find in *Laborem Exercens*). Taken together, he concludes, all three concerns are limits observed in order to more favorably orient the human toward the kingdom of God, which is the basic template for the human life, well-lived.[5]

Laborem exercens is John Paul II's third encyclical, as *Caritas in veritate* (2009) is Benedict XVI's third encyclical. But their symmetry is not merely numeric. Both are the third movement in a theme of the papacies of John Paul II and Benedict XVI, following more fundamental encyclicals. And each of these treats a theme from the Christian life in a more concrete and particular fashion, bringing to fruition the theological and anthropological visions set down earlier, springing from very specific concrete circumstances, though they paint on a broader canvas. For John Paul, the very concrete situation of his own Polish roots and his own role in the political transformation of that country animates his direct address to workers in *Laborem exercens*. So too does *Caritas in veritate*, turning to the role of the human in specific areas of social and political life, move from the notion of the common good to specific applications of this, making it clear that that common good "is primarily effected through institutions."[6]

These institutions, however, must be humane, promoting just work environments. Drew Christiansen reports that Benedict fears that most of these corporations are developed in the form of a structure that is basically a "binary model of market-plus-State,"[7] in Benedict's words, "almost exclusively answerable to their investors, thereby limiting their social value."[8] Against this model, Christiansen notes that *Caritas in Veritate* contains "the strongest endorsement of workers' right to organize" since *Rerum Novarum*.[9] Yet Benedict is well aware of the disparities between political and corporate entities. He knows well that multinational corporations are, because of their holdings in many countries, now able to wield an influence denied to many nations, which also attenuates the ability of a union to organize, given the mobility of a globalized workforce. This comes home in a direct fashion when one hears a familiar complaint about a chain discount store putting a beloved mom-and-pop place out of business, at the same time that the mail brings the news of a drop in one's retirement account (whose mix of funds depends in part upon the price per share of the same chain discount store). All of our interests, not merely those of the multinationals, are now globalized.

Women in the workforce as consumers and caretakers

The closing exhortation text views its audience as "working men, who are the chief artisans of the prodigious changes which the world is undergoing today." As with the other exhortations, the sensibility of the 1960's assumed that most "workers" were male as, it was also assumed, were the other groups addressed by the exhortation: "artists" and "thinkers" and "rulers" (and, thus the separate exhortation for women, many of whom were, in fact, working in 1965). Even if the scale is limited to work done outside the home, a majority of women work today, as the percentage of adult women in the United States working outside the home has almost tripled since 1900, when about 19 percent of women of working age were employed.[10] In 2010, 58.6 percent of working age women were employed, comprising 47 percent of workers in the United States. This percentage has remained fairly stable for the last decade.

In spite of these numbers, while Catholic support for male workers has consistently been strong, support for women in the workforce—and particularly for wages for women in the workforce—has been mixed at best. (For some reason, Catholics do not think of women religious as being in the workforce; for these we seem to have had a full employment program, as my fourth grade classroom had seven rows of desks, eight desks per row—and one low-wage sister/teacher at the head of the room.) Christine Hinze, in a thorough survey of the "living wage" discussion throughout the twentieth century, notes the need to distinguish between traditional Catholic support for workers and families and the understanding of gender that forms the backdrop to that support, as well the need to read both issues in the context of differing social norms.[11] Typical of that support for workers were the efforts of Msgr. John Ryan, Catholic champion of the living wage in the early twentieth century, who argued that all men need to make a "family living wage," not merely an "individual wage," because wages should allow, structurally, for the good of families. For Ryan, women should be entitled to an individual wage, but this need was understood to be provisional, soon to be eclipsed by marriage.[12] The notion of a "just wage," as such emerges from the presumed

132

negation between a wage earner and an employer, requires, Ryan found, an understanding of what a reasonable standard of living might entail, according to a given time and place—and for Ryan, that standard was the nuclear family with a breadwinning father.

This analysis is not adequate today, if it ever was. In the contemporary context, Hinze finds that, in "portraying the normative economic role of the husband as wage-earning breadwinner active in the public workplace, and of the housewife as shopper-consumer ensconced in the household (an image that conceals the economic and social value of unpaid domestic labor), the family living wage agenda *updated*, for a mass consumer society, the ideology of 'separate spheres' that accompanied the rise of modern industrialized market economy."[13] In short, women's primary role in this imagined but powerfully resonant scenario reduces their contribution to the economy all too quickly to "shopping." By consuming and through patterns of consumption, women mark how their families will be positioned in culture—what their children's opportunities are, who the family will meet, how they will understand themselves. Yet, as in 1965—though to a greater extent—women still are working outside the home, now in every industry there is. This is certainly cheered and supported by magisterial statements, though it is still seen as an afterthought, an add-on; whether this should impact theology and anthropology remains to be seen—we have "working women," but adding "working" to "men" sounds odd. Moreover, in an economy in which health care plays an ever-larger role, women figure in that realm, again, precisely as consumers, as the primary contact and decision-maker in the household—they decide who's sick, they juggle the appointments, they wait for the doctor to call back and, in a health care era of "outpatient procedures," women are more likely to be the ones taking the groggy patient home, stopping at the drug store for Percocet and deciding whether the amount of bleeding and pain is normal or not. Women deliver the majority of unpaid care, whether to their own children with extraordinary needs, their spouses or their parents, often while holding down a "real" job: "[t]he average caregiver is age 46, female, married and working outside the home earning an annual income of $35,000."[14] That worker making $35,000 a year, moreover, is likely to have a job with little autonomy and flexibility. For her, caregiving comes with a high personal cost.

I still recall bringing my youngest to a meeting while she was still a baby. I wasn't in charge of the meeting, I just needed to be there, so I bundled Margaret into the stroller, brought a bottle and sat near the door. All was well, she gurgled a bit and slept and everyone thought this was great. What I noticed, though, was the secretary who joined the meeting to take notes for the search committee. Women and men faculty at my university have a lot of latitude as new parents; there is parental leave, and it is quite routine to work one's teaching schedule around parental duties. University staff, on the other hand, have parental leave, but it is carefully clocked, and then the usual work schedule takes over. I thought about that secretary as I sat in the meeting. Having a faculty member bring in her new baby to the meeting was adorable; the same move by a staff member would be unthinkable. There's a reason I make more money than she does and have a private office rather than cubicle space. But I'm not sure why my "working mother" status is continually, publicly, privileged, while her status as a "working mother" is considered a personal issue.

At life's end, with an ever-increasing aging population, the calculus of caregiving continues. Their status as caregivers has an extraordinary impact on women's lifetime wages, with the final impact being felt as they have often not prepared well for their own needs as they themselves age. This has some parallels to the global situation as, in developing countries, women are very likely to be the ones cultivating crops (to feed others), but extremely unlikely to own land (which one can rent out in old age). This is the current situation of women in the workforce; their labor merits income, but they are not seen when the topic shifts to wealth. Both income and wealth are factors in the growing disparity of resources.

The major issue for women in the workforce is that, while the personal is certainly political, the reverse is true as well: policy statements, economic structures, systems of employment and financial systems all conspire to yield benefits and burdens that are always also profoundly personal. Women function in this workforce both as consumers and as caretakers, in systems that reproduce themselves in ideals about female power, sexuality, and obligation.

Immigration

The status of immigrant labor most directly links the question of work and social ethics, with those who write about immigrants to the United States often using the image of the border to evoke the powerful complex of policy and land and aspiration and desperation in play.[15] While migration also occurs for ecological, cultural or political reasons, for most immigrants the lure of the border is the promise of work or better-paying work, or they come to the border as unwilling workers or along the way become victims of force, indentured or enslaved or trafficked. Indeed, Kristen Heyer reports that "Catholic Relief Services-Mexico now estimates that more than 70% of women attempting to cross the border are sexually exploited enroute."[16] These borders, however, are a factor not only in the lives of migrant peoples; they shape the experience of the population of the host country to a profound effect. Which is not to say the experience of immigration for migrants or hosts is uniform; to the contrary, while the United States receives the largest raw number of migrants per year, countries in the Middle East (Qatar, UAE, Kuwait) receive the greatest number proportionate to the home population.[17]

Aware of the social, economic and political complexity involved, Heyer therefore argues for an analysis of the notion of "social sin" with regard to migrant peoples as now necessary for a consideration of what any work might mean in a global context. Heyer also argues that the dialog about immigration, particularly the migration of undocumented people to the United States, pits a call for laws focused on individual action against peoples who are experiencing a situation that is broken at a level beyond individual culpability. The emphasis on individual action is typical of the sense of justice owned by many in the United States and codified in its laws, but this emphasis runs counter to many threads in the New Testament[18] and is, finally, inadequate to the complex situation of immigrants. Gregory Baum's sociological grounding offers, Heyer suggests, elements for an appropriately theological ethic, taking account of "unjust institutions and dehumanizing trends," "cultural and religious ideologies" that can distort the ability to discern the good, and the resulting "collective decisions made by distorted consciousness" that increases social and cultural pathology.[19] From these, Heyer develops a notion of social sin as an analytical tool for the discussion of a Christian response to the challenge of undocumented immigrants.

Heyer finds liberation theology's methodological insistence on the preferential option for the poor to offer the most fully-developed resources for this Christian response. But the resources of liberation theology are still under suspicion at the highest level of Church authority. This wariness can be seen in John Paul II's fixation on the danger, in contemporary discourse, of a loss of the sense of individual sin. He expresses concern about an approach that "contrasts social sin and personal sin, not without ambiguity, in a way that leads more or less unconsciously to the *watering down and almost the abolition of personal sin*, with the recognition only of social guilt and responsibilities." The pontiff concludes that "[t]he real responsibility, then, lies with individuals."[20] In particular, John Paul II names liberation theology to be vulnerable to such a "watering down."[21]

But when we consider the numerous economic and cultural factors that drive immigrants to cross borders, the neat breakdown of individual versus social sin is not only inaccurate, but can serve as a convenient means of avoiding the real moral issues raised for individual Christians by the social situation that gives rise to the plight of undocumented immigrants. Reflecting this, we find a genuinely social approach that sounds very much like liberation theology to be illustrated, in a text that also engages the question of human culpability, in a recent letter to immigrants, written by the Hispanic/Latino bishops of the United States:

> In your suffering faces we see the true face of Jesus Christ. We are well aware of the great sacrifice you make for your families' well-being. Many of you perform the most difficult jobs and receive miserable salaries and no health insurance or social security. Despite your contributions to the well-being of our country, instead of receiving our thanks, you are often treated as criminals because you have violated current immigration laws.
>
> We are also very aware of the pain suffered by those families who have experienced the deportation of one of

their members. We are conscious of the frustration of youth and young adults who have grown up in this country and whose dreams are shattered because they lack legal immigration status. We also know of the anxiety of those whose application process for permanent residency is close to completion and of the anguish of those who live daily under the threat of deportation. This situation cries out to God for a worthy and humane solution....[22]

This pastoral statement traces, with great clarity, the genuinely dehumanizing effects of the current system of laws and deterrents, while recognizing the drive for work that propels individual workers, as moral agents (often, we note, on behalf of their families), into this situation. Heyer's ethic, informed by liberation theology, names this social sin for what it is, and calls individuals to join forces in the service of a systemic and socially-conscious response. The presence of undocumented workers is a social issue not only for those workers and their employers, but for all whose employment and consumption patterns is systematically interconnected with their labor.

Globalization and subsidiarity

A similar tone, that recognizes the border-crossing involved in all questions of work and worker justice, is sounded by Lisa Cahill's analysis of *Caritas in Veritate*. Cahill finds that this document genuinely grasps the plurality of the global situation as it demonstrates both Benedict's hope for a heightened profile for the United Nations as a way to bring about effective and socially just structures, and his clear acknowledgement "that the universal common good can be neither unitary nor advanced by a cohesive world authority."[23] The latter, Cahill observes, represents a new moment in papal statements on the subject of global governance, one that allows its empirical variety to stand, rather than reducing it by abstraction.

Such an approach, that recognizes the role that systems play in the presence or absence of justice, is a departure from Benedict's earlier writing on Jesus (as Joseph Ratzinger) and in his first encyclical, *Deus caritas est*. In both of these, structural change took a back seat to personal acts of human charity, motivated by Christian faith.[24] Benedict, Cahill suggests, is more comfortable with shades of gray in the global realm while his theological framework and the understanding of European Christianity that is closely tied to it, remains fixed in more traditional categories: "[t]he various political commitments that Benedict now envisions as proper to the Church have yet to be integrated into a Christology and ecclesiology that are adequate to their scope."[25]

This recognition of the increasing complexity of the situation of any worker is necessary for a responsible moral analysis. Those who have work must engage with the conditions that make this possible, often conditions of material privilege, or family connections or—it must be said—luck, in the sense of raw good fortune. Miroslav Volf's reminder that Christians must build concrete support for the poor into their standard of living is appropriate to remember here, as it insists that the possibility of the loss of work be part of the structural calculus. What is at issue, though, is how to account for those underemployed or unemployed or whose work does not pay enough for their dependents. At what point to their needs become a structural factor?

Here we turn to the question of how the principle of subsidiarity informs the social justice tradition of the Church. *Subsidiarity*, as a principle of social policy, simply means that issues should be worked through at the lowest level possible, but also at the highest level necessary. Subsidiarity is a necessary regulating principle between the individual and large social units, such as a state, which has as its goal the solicitude for the broadest popular participation, while recognizing that some issues can and should be a function of higher levels of government. Benedict, we observed above, already recognizes the "primary" role of institutions in the achievement of the common good: a sound and comprehensive healthcare policy can do far more good than a coffee can by the cash register with a pleading note. For Catholic theology in general, subsidiarity is a necessary corollary to hierarchy, in that subsidiarity ensures that the specific places found in a complex organization have their own integrity. For the question of the global Church, for example, subsidiarity means that decisions about how the Church should operate in a given culture should be made directly at the level of the culture in question, with enough "oversight" (at the episcopal level, and sometimes in national bodies of bishops) to ensure communion. Finding that point of integrity for any given question, I suggest, requires a nuanced understanding of both catholicity and hierarchy.[26] Subsidiarity is important for an understanding of catholicity—the Church's understanding of tradition in history as having both a horizontal and vertical dimension—because of the church's emphasis on intermediary institutions, something in play in *Caritas in Veritate*. Non-governmental organizations (NGOs), for example, cannot simply be seen as isolated charitable units, rather, the work of any given NGO it is effective only if integrated (which need not mean that this integration is totalizing) into the local political and economic structure. Benedict's advance in *Caritas in Veritate* lies in the recognition of the catholicity of these structures, with subsidiarity, as yeast, pushing both upward and downward as a social stabilizer. Such an understanding of subsidiarity should also inform any analysis of women's roles as consumers and caregivers, because of the profoundly influential social function of these two roles in the larger economic, social and cultural picture. Such an understanding of subsidiarity should also inform the social analysis of the "illegal" immigrant worker, precisely in his or her status as "undocumented."

In a similar vein, we recognize that the goods of the world are not, finally, private property. Writing in honor of Paul VI's *Populorum Progressio*, John Paul, in *Solicitudo Rei Socialis*, points to "the characteristic principle of Christian social doctrine: the goods of this world are originally meant for all."[27] He grants the usefulness of the notion of private property but, listening carefully to his use of "originally" in this text, it is clear that he refuses to see "the goods of this world" merely as individual things. Rather, he claims, "[p]rivate property, in fact, is under a "social mortgage.""[28] In this sense, our use of the "goods of this world" must conform to an implicit recognition of subsidiarity, including those "goods" we claim as payment for our work.

For the consideration of work and workers, then, a strong sense of globalization and subsidiarity can serve as a way of situating agency: I can't do everything; I must do something. What will that mean? What must I do? If work has to do with our public accountability in the world, then, somehow, to work justly we must have a de facto understanding of subsidiarity that is operative in our orientation. Why should *I* do *this*?

Work as co-operative grace

> The Church is ever seeking to understand you better. But on your part you must endeavor to understand what the Church means for you, working men, who are the chief artisans of the prodigious changes which the world is undergoing today. For you know full well that unless a mighty spiritual inspiration animates these changes, they will cause disaster for humanity instead of bringing it happiness.[29]

The Catholic Church, simply because of the reach of its extensive corps of diplomatic missions, its charitable structures on the ground in all corners of the world, and its polyvalent relations with numerous non-governmental organizations, has as a privilege and duty to comment on the fullness of human life and work as found in a variety of economic systems. We should welcome this commentary and welcome partnerships between ecclesial and other groups that engage freely in these dialogs. Central to this conversation is the invitation of *Gaudium et Spes*, which turns the face of the Church toward the world, claiming that, for Catholic Christians, "nothing genuinely human fails to raise an echo in their hearts."[1]

This breadth must be borne in mind as, with *Laborem exercens*, Richard McCormick observes, we find a new approach to social questions, "as if John Paul II is inviting us to share an ongoing philosophical meditation with him."[30] The tone invites experience to test theory; it proposes a way of thinking together without laying down a "social doctrine"; the inductive is prized over the deductive. This appropriate modesty about conclusions is necessary as the texts in the social teaching of the Church are compared side by side, and reveal the different presuppositions, social and political contexts, and personal histories of their various authors.[31] While such modesty is appropriate, McCormick also notes the tendency, in magisterial documents, to eschew the expertise of the laity. Curiously, in our own day, when policy questions are deemed to be issues appropriate for prudential judgment, that judgment is often received with a spirit of absolute relativism. In other words, those things that are considered appropriate for the judgment of skilled lay persons—questions of social policy or wage structures—are seen as producing conclusions that have no force whatsoever.

One grants that the social-political-economic context for a consideration of how we work and what we do is enormously complex. On a day-to-day level this is "simplified" only by the difficulty in finding and retaining any specific job. It is clear that the labor force, and the notion of work itself, is going through wrenching changes even as, to different degrees in different countries and regions, the overall global picture continues to be one of a rising overall standard of living for many and net progress when considering innovations that will be of social benefit. Nevertheless, a new precariousness threatens as, in many specific places, market swings threaten to overwhelm the local or regional economic system before it can "right itself." A sense of this anxiety undergirds one commentator's observation; about the roots of the current employment slump in the United States: "[i]t's a problem rooted in the kinds of jobs we have, the kind we need, and the kind we're losing, and rooted as well in the kind of workers we want and the kind we don't know what to do with."[32] Regardless of the point of analysis, workers today wonder not only if they will lose their jobs but, on a more existential level, if the kind of person they are will continue to be useful in a rapidly-changing world.

At the same time, it seems significant that, *pace* the various Occupy protests, most Americans seem to have resigned themselves to living with or not noticing a widening economic gap, a context that profoundly shapes our understanding of work and its (always relative) value. What would have to happen to change this is unclear. It is also not clear that that this gap is viewed as merely one option among many for a successful social and economic order for, as Alan Krueger observes, "Income inequality is a policy choice."[33] It is also true, however, that even carefully-cultivated policies can have a variety of impacts, some not foreseeable. For example, the wide availability of subprime mortgages encouraged low-income families, often racial minorities, to take on housing costs they could not afford. The (poorly-communicated) financial risk of these mortgages came with the obvious social benefit of a move from high-poverty areas to middle-income, less racially-segregated communities of home owners. But when the financial crisis hit, Richard Rothstein at the Economic Policy Institute observed, this social progress evaporated: "Foreclosures on homes financed or re-financed with subprime loans have led to the displacement of many minority families from more stable communities, forcing their return to more racially isolated and poorer neighborhoods."[34]

So why would these families take this risk? Is it simply a matter of over-reach, or was it a calculated risk? Consider this: Even in our seemingly merit-based system of higher education, it is clear that social context matters in moving ahead. In 2005, a study by the College Board (the group that produces and administers the SAT) "found that among those scoring highest in math tests in 1992, just under three-quarters of students from families in the highest quartile went on to get bachelor's degrees by the year 2000. Among those from families in the bottom quartile, less than half that number, 29 percent, went on to get degrees."[35] In other words, a significant number of mathematically-talented students did not prepare to join the workforce at the level they should, seemingly because the social or cultural or political network they required to follow through with college was not available. This situation is also "a policy choice."

Policy choices are in play, too, in the way that we understand "work" in the Church in the United States. While official texts have recognized the value of lay ministry, there is still a sense that such ministry is understood, *de facto*, as "extraordinary," an accommodation that is less than ideal. As long as this nostalgic attitude persists, parish ministers will always have low pay and no job security, and professionalism will not happen *on either side*. Certainly lay ministers feel keenly that they are overly dependent on the whims of clergy, their employment a function of the pastor assigned to a given parish. It is possible that this lack of recognition of lay ministry also, in ways that may be less recognized, hampers clergy as well, as there is no clear provision for the status of the parish team when the pastor is reassigned. Perhaps priests and bishops feel con-strained by personnel decisions they did not make, perhaps these blurred lines of responsibility are why clergy handle their executive functions awkwardly and, seemingly, insensitively. Remaining in this provisional situation is yet another policy choice.

All of these policy choices, however, are set against a backdrop of our understanding of human agency which, for the Christian, must not be reduced to material inputs—any more than the Christian can regard the inputs themselves as "merely" material. In other words, we do not "make" meaning;[36] all human work, as it engages with Creation itself, is an intentional act of cooperative grace.[37] While we do know things by their effects, no work is solely *self*-expressive; its expression is always more than that. The anthro-pological question of work and working has, therefore, the sense that it begins always "in medias res"; because it takes place within the unfolding liturgy of salvation history, it unfolds within the sacramentality of human life.

Thus does Jesuit Agbonkhianmeghe Orobator find much of value for the African context in *Caritas in veritate*'s address of the problem of an "anthropological poverty,"[38] in which the dignity of work is lost because the human being has not in the first place been addressed in the fullness of human personhood. He suggests, more-over, a more capacious understanding of "nature"; one that draws on a more nuanced understanding of the African interdependent sense of humanity and ecology, one that would better recognize that human beings are "constituted 'not only by matter but also by spirit.'"[39] This finds resonance in Hanby's claim that *merely* ensur-ing political and economic rights for workers is not "sufficient to ensure the integrity of work in its subjective sense…[rather,] there is an ineliminably 'aesthetic' dimension to the quest for social jus tice."[40] I agree with Hanby, but I still need to see the money; such an aesthetic dimension must not remain abstract, with political and economic rights put on ice while we work out the beauty question, because this aesthetic dimension is received, rejoiced in and redemptively engaged only through the concrete instantiation of "ordinary" "material" persons. At work.

We must also be aware of the construction of systems that eliminate altogether the role of the human in their execution. By definition, such systems will produce dehumanized results. These systems may be mechanical, but they can also be automated processes, or even (seemingly human) communication structures, as anyone who has undergone a "re-organization" of their workplace realizes as they scan the new flow-chart and realize, heart sinking, that they are now redundant. With an implicit nod to Marshall McLuhan ("the medium is the message"), George Grant notes that the forms of our communication tend to dictate the parameters of our inquiry; "when we are deliberating in any practical situation our judgment rather acts like a mirror, which throws back the very metaphysic of the technology which we are supposed to be deliberating about in detail."[41] Grant does not argue against technology in itself; we need these systems, we need their precision, we need their speed—sometimes, yes, the best surgeon will be a robot. But the human scale, the human value, of our systems matter; our systems are not "impartial" forms of data-gathering or de-contextualized forms of "assessment."

For the economic system, the lure of the objective "dollar" or "euro" or "peso" is a particular issue; money seems so (deceptively) clean, so unencumbered. Thus we get things like financial instruments that operate exclusively within their own logic, and *therefore* produce the de-contextualized logic of the "credit default swap," a financial instrument that games a system that presumes failure. As Hanby observes, "[t]he instruments we have made to serve us have re-made us and our culture in their image."[42] In other words, we do both create and become our instruments, which is why we must not hand over our humanity in favor of materially-perfect execution.

On the other hand, some humility is required all around. Sometimes these systems do—in their ungraspable mechanics— offer genuinely new information. They constructively critique their creators (humans, at work) in ways that provide new information about being human or even in ways that present genuine novelty for and about the human future we are living into. We are, we all know, living in a moment when we can create systems that transcend themselves, systems that can, potentially, either swamp or bootstrap our ongoing labor with God.

In conclusion, I would like to reverse my assignment from the "closing exhortation" and offer a practical exhortation from the laity to our bishops and parish priests: stand with us as we all work. See your own work as more like ours than not. It will not violate the difference we all recognize between clergy and laity to emphasize more clearly our bonds as workers who labor at tasks we apply for or inherit or simply are assigned by the world. Recognize that the lay people who fill church pews have jobs that, like yours, call for sacrifice and fidelity: the foreman for a commercial construction site, the head nurse for an intensive care unit, a financial officer for a large urban public school system, a parent of a child with special needs, or a mid-level computer expert whose task it is to ensure that the server is working 24/7. These jobs, like yours, require great devotion and singleness of purpose. Stand with us in the world of work, share with us that sometimes your tasks for our Church are tedious, that you feel pulled between competing goods, that you feel inadequate and that yes, you know could have handled the "kerfluffle" in the liturgy meeting last week with less drama. We understand; these are things we all face as workers. Stand with us in our shared world of work as our co-laborers, and we will learn from one another.

And in the great liturgy we will all do our best work; we will make ourselves into one people, called to *ora et labora*, a life of love that gives rise to labor and labor that is love incarnate, a life together, that will ultimately join the angels in a single act of praise.[43]

Dr. Nancy Dallavalle *is Associate Professor and Chair of the Department of Religious Studies at Fairfield University in Fairfield, CT.*

DISCUSSION QUESTIONS

1. "Economic inequality is a policy choice," says Alan Kruger. He is commenting on the extreme inequity in some sectors of the current U.S. economy, but the inequality he observes is a constant of human history, though it was not always recognized as a policy choice. How is it that we have come to "choose" economic inequality? What do we do keep this inequity in place? Are there other options? What choices would make those other options possible?

2. If we develop a theology of work, does this not also suppose a theology of unemployment or underemployment? How would we describe this dynamism over the life of the human person?

3. Is there part of your own work (considering not only paid employment but also parenting or home maintenance) that is tedious or boring? Is there a part of your own work that is demoralizing or painful? How do you regard that aspect of working?
4. Might Catholic Christians and Protestant Christians regard work differently, given the different perspectives they traditionally bring to an understanding of the role of grace in human life? What resources might each of these traditions offer? To which experiences of work do each speak best?

SUGGESTED READINGS

Benedict XVI, Encyclical, *Caritas In Veritate*. 2009, http://www.vatican.va/holy_father/benedict_xvi/encyclicals/documents/hf_ben-xvi_enc_20090629_caritas-in-veritate_en.html.

Lewis H. Lapham, "The Servant Problem," *Lapham's Quarterly*, Spring 2011, http://www.laphamsquarterly.org/preamble/the-servant-problem.php?page=all.

John Paul II. Encyclical. *Laborem Exercens*. 1981, http://www.vatican.va/holy_father/john_paul_ii/encyclicals/documents/hf_jp-ii_enc_14091981_laborem-exercens_en.html.

National Conference of Catholic Bishops (now the USCCB): Economic Justice for All: Pastoral Letter on Catholic Social Teaching and the U.S. Economy. 1986, http://www.usccb.org/upload/economic_justice_for_all.pdf.

Kathleen Norris, *The Quotidian Mysteries: Laundry, Liturgy and "Women's Work"* (Madeleva Lecture in Spirituality. Mahwah NJ: Paulist Press, 1998).

Miroslav Volf, "God at Work," *Word & World* 25 (2005): 381-93.

NOTES

1. http://www.npr.org/templates/story/story.php?storyId=5391395.

2. The best illustration for this interpenetration of social justice and work is the status of labor unions. In the United States, in particular (the situation is slightly different in Europe), labor unions have been supported by the Catholic Church as instruments

of social good. See Jan P. Schotte, CICM, "The Social Teaching of the Church: *Laborem exercens*, A New Challenge," *Review of Social Economy* 40 (1982): 340-59, and Patricia Ann Lamoureaux, "A Theological Ethic for Renewing Church-Labor Alliance," *Horizons* 30 (2003): 67-91.

3. Miroslav Volf, "On Human Work: An Evaluation of the Key Ideas of the Encyclical *Laborem Exercens*," *Scottish Journal of Theology* 37 (1984): 68.

4. Volf, "On Human Work," 69.

5. Volf, "On Human Work," 77-79.

6. Drew Christiansen, SJ, "Metaphysics and Society: A Commentary on Caritas in Veritate," *Theological Studies* 71 (2010): 13.

7. Christensen, "Metaphysics and Society," 21.

8. *Caritas in veritate* 40, cited in Christiansen, "Metaphysics and Society," 21.

9. Christensen, "Metaphysics and Society," 24.

10. http://www.bls.gov/opub/cwc/cm20030124ar02p1.htm. The statistics from 1900, of course, may not fully reflect the labor participation rate of poor and/or minority women; the latter in particular are likely not to have been accurately counted.

11. Christine Firer Hinze, "U.S. Catholic Social Thought, Gender, and Economic Livelihood," *Theological Studies* 66 (2005): 570.

12. Patricia Ann Lamoureux, "Justice for Wage Earners: Retrieving Insights from the Catholic Community," *Horizons* 28 (2001): 220.

13. Hinze, "U.S. Catholic Social Thought, Gender, and Economic Livelihood," 74.

14. http://www.caregiver.org/caregiver/jsp/content_node.jsp?nodeid=892.

15. *Gaudium et Spes* [66] warns: "When workers come from another country or district and contribute to the economic advancement of a nation or region by their labor, all discrimination as regards wages and working conditions must be carefully avoided. All the people, moreover, above all the public authorities, must treat them not as mere tools of production but as persons, and must help them to bring their families to live with them and to provide themselves with a decent dwelling; they must also see to it that

these workers are incorporated into the social life of the country or region that receives them."

16. Erica Dahl-Bredine, Country Manager, Catholic Relief Services—Mexico Program, personal report to visiting delegation, Tucson. May 22, 2009; cited in Kristin Heyer, "Social Sin and Immigration: Good Fences Make Bad Neighbors," *Theological Studies* 71 (2010): 431.

17. http://www.migrationinformation.org/datahub/compara tive.cfm#worldstats.

18. Heyer, "Social Sin and Immigration," 414.

19. Heyer, "Social Sin and Immigration," 426.

20. Heyer, "Social Sin and Immigration," 416, quoting John Paul II, *Reconciliatio et paenitentia* no. 16, Apostolic Exhortation of December 2, 1984 (Heyer's emphasis).

21. See Heyer, "Social Sin and Immigration," 421, n. 48.

22. "Letter of the Hispanic/Latino Bishops to Immigrants," Monday, December 12, 2011. http://usccbmedia.blogspot.com/2011/12/estas-son-las-mananitasof-hispanic_12.html.

23. Lisa Sowle Cahill, "*Caritas in Veritate*: Benedict's Global Reorientation," *Theological Studies* 71 (2010): 310.

24. Cahill, "*Caritas in Veritate*," 297.

25. Cahill, "*Caritas in Veritate*," 317.

26. See also the discussion in Kent A. Van Til, "Subsidiarity and Sphere-Sovereignty: A Match Made In...?" *Theological Studies* 69 (2008): 610-36.

27. The text of *Solicitudo* traces this point to St. Thomas Aquinas, *Summa Theol.* IIa IIae, q. 66, art. 2. For example, "...man ought to possess external things, not as his own, but as common, so that, to wit, he is ready to communicate them to others in their need."

28. *Solicitudo Rei Socialis*, 42.

29. "To Workers."

30. Richard A. McCormick, "Notes on Moral Theology: 1981," *Theological Studies* 43 (1982): 94.

31. McCormick draws this insight from the work of John Coleman who, according to McCormick, makes the point that "history will not bear out the contention that in social teaching there is an unbroken coherent unity untouched by the waves of time." McCormick, "Notes on Moral Theology," 98.

32. www.vanityfair.com/politics/2012/01/stiglitz-depression-201201.

33. http://www.epi.org/blog/income-inequality-policy-choice-alan-krueger-speech/.

34. http://www.epi.org/publication/subprime-loan-debacle-intensified-segregation/.

35. http://trends.collegeboard.org/downloads/archives/EP_2005_Update.pdf; cited in http://campaignstops.blogs.nytimes.com/2012/03/12/the-reproduction-of-privilege.

36. Michael Hanby, "*Homo Faber und/or Homo Adorans*: On the Place of Human Making in a Sacramental Cosmos," *Communio* 38 (2011): 210.

37. "Ancient *téchnê* presupposes and works within an anterior order of nature that is given, hence the suggestion that art bears a relation to nature analogous to grace, perfecting rather than destroying nature. Receptivity to this order is what it means to say that thought commences in wonder." Hanby, "*Homo Faber* and/or *Homo Adorans*," 212.

38. Agbonkhianmeghe E. Orobator, SJ, "*Caritas in Veritate* and Africa's Burden of (Under)Development," *Theological Studies* 71 (2010): 323.

39. Orobator, "*Caritas in Veritate*," 326, citing CV 48.

40. Hanby, "*Homo Faber* and/or *Homo Adorans*," 220.

41. George Grant, Technology and Justice (Concord, Ontario: Anasi Press, 1986), 32, cited in Hanby, "*Homo Faber* and/or *Homo Adorans*," 218.

42. Hanby, "*Homo Faber* and/or *Homo Adorans*," 232.

43. Hanby, "*Homo Faber* and/or *Homo Adorans*," 214. See also Benedict XVI, "The Origins of Western Theology and the Roots of European Culture," Paris, 12 September 2008 [http://www.zenit.org/article-23606?l=english].

To Women and Men of Science

Science, Spirituality and Vatican II

John F. Haught

In 1612 the poet John Donne composed "Anatomie of the World," in which these anxious lines appear:

> And new Philosophy calls all in doubt,
> The Element of fire is quite put out;
> The Sun is lost, and th'earth, and no man's wit
> Can well direct him where to looke for it.
> 'Tis all in peeces, all coherence gone…(1611-12)

Two years earlier Galileo Galilei, whom the poet may have met in Padua, had published the first scientific bestseller, *The Starry Messenger*. This was Galileo's first public announcement that the heavens are not organized the way most people had thought. A half century earlier (in 1543) Nicolaus Copernicus had already made the sun change places with "th'earth," but not too many people had taken him seriously. Those who paid attention at all interpreted Copernicus's new model as a "hypothesis," useful for making astronomical measurements and predictions, but not representative of the real world. Galileo, however, was less tentative. For him the Copernican system is not a hypothesis but an accurate representation of the way things are.

Donne's lyrics express the religious anxiety that has occurred more than once when the cosmological setting presupposed by a religious worldview is turned topsy-turvy. For many Christians and other religious people today, for example, nothing has destroyed the apparent coherence of nature more dramatically than developments in biology over the last century and a half. Taken together with geology and Big Bang cosmology, Charles Darwin's science has rattled the faith of many Christians. Science's ragged evolutionary portrayal of life is not what they had come to expect from their Creator. The high degree of randomness, the reckless impersonality of natural selection and the immensity of time required for the gradual emergence of living diversity has shattered the benign simplicity of previous conceptions of natural order. Just as Donne felt spiritually disoriented at losing his spatial grounding, so people today wonder how to connect their spirituality to the immensity of time and a constantly changing universe. The question of science and spirituality is as alive and important today as ever.

Spirituality involves at the very least the quest for something to which we can lift up our hearts, something that can give us a "zest for living."[1] For centuries the geocentric model of the universe had functioned as a sacrament of divine perfection while ancient Greek philosophy provided a powerful conceptual setting for the lifting up of hearts. The perfectly circular movement of the heavenly spheres and the faultless spherical geometry of the sun and moon offered at least a hint of the perfection that exists beyond our shadowy world. So fixed was the assumption that perfect circularity is essential to a universe created by a perfect God that even Galileo could not give up this ancient assumption.

The "new philosophy"—by which Donne means the Copernican revolution—called "all in doubt." With the newer measurements of celestial motion by early modern astronomers the heavens underwent a series of demotions that eventually blunted their capacity to symbolize the perfection people needed to anchor their spiritual lives. The birth of modern science initiated a seismic upheaval in spiritual life, and we are still feeling the aftershocks.

In the ancient world Aristotle had portrayed the heavens as a quintessential (fifth) kind of reality far surpassing in value the four mundane elements—earth, air, fire and water. But Tycho Brahe (1546-1601) demonstrated to his shocked contemporaries that comets and supernovas—both implying change and novelty—existed beyond the moon in the domain of supposedly unchanging perfection. Johannes Kepler (1571-1630) calculated that planets move in "ugly" ellipses rather than perfectly circular orbits. And

Galileo (1564-1642), looking at the skies through his newly upgraded telescope, delivered the final blow to the assumption of astronomical perfection. Venus, he discovered, goes through phases. It changes dramatically over time. Jupiter has satellites that orbit not around Earth but around an extraterrestrial heavenly body. And, most disturbing, Galileo saw that the most excellent heavenly body of all, the sun, is blemished by what we now call sunspots. The heavens are not "quintessential" after all. "The Element of fire is quite put out," and the principle of mediocrity now applies to all visible things both beyond and beneath the moon.

Where then, in the age of science, can our spiritual quest locate any symbols of perfection in creation that may stir us even now to lift up our hearts? Where in nature are there sacraments of perfection that can animate our own lives and give us hope? Is there now any equivalent of the flawless heavens that in ages past pointed so palpably to the infinite?

Can science help us in this search? Scientific method, after all, thrives on the belief that what seems remarkable at first is, underneath it all, quite ordinary. To the scientific naturalist everything in nature is ultimately explainable in terms of mundane material units and invariant physical laws. According to the acclaimed scientist and author Peter Atkins, whatever in nature appeals initially to our sacramental or romantic sensibilities, is *really* nothing more than physical simplicity "masquerading as complexity."[2]

So, now that nature, to many educated people, seems unremarkable at best and deeply flawed at worst, is there anything in the scientific understanding of nature that can point us once again in the direction of a perfection that can arouse a throb of joy in our hearts and charge us with a new zest for living?

Yes. The universe, as we can now see, is still coming into being, and our own existence is part of an enormous and still unfinished epic of creation. This new picture of the universe has enormous implications for spirituality. Science has opened up before us a fourteen-billion-year-old cosmic *story* that may now provide a fresh setting for our spiritual aspirations. Scientific discoveries, as we have learned in the last two centuries, clearly imply that nature is narrative to the core. The story is not yet finished, and if it is not yet finished it may still hold the promise of new creation up ahead.

By unveiling a four-billion-year-old journey of life in a fourteen-billion-year-old cosmic drama, science now makes it possible for us realistically to lift up our hearts, not just to the heavens above but also toward the mysteriously dawning future of Creation that lies up ahead. The new cosmic story is one onto which we may now map our faith and hope in the biblical God of promise. Not only Abraham, Israel and the Church but also the whole universe is being called into a new future, and we along with it. Together with Abraham, the prophets and Jesus we can taste the kingdom of God not so much through direct contemplation of an eternal present, nor in nostalgia for an imagined past state of primordial cosmic perfection, but primarily through anticipation of a new future for the whole of the cosmos. We look forward not to another world but to the new creation of this one.

Gaudium et Spes

Christian faith is inseparable from hope for new creation, and one of the great recent instances of such hope, I believe, was the stirring in Pope John XXIII's heart and mind as he sought to open the windows of the Church to let in fresh air. A new sense of the future was present also in Vatican II and, before that, in biblical and theological studies that influenced the Council's invitation to renew our Christian faith. Many of us who were around when the Council took place can never forget the sense that a new future was breaking into our world during that period. A half-century later we still draw strength from the mood of expectation that for many of us seemed comparable to the wave of hope that swept over the ancient world with the first coming of Christianity. The Council left us with a deeper conviction than ever that Christianity is essentially forward-looking and that our God, in the words of theologian Karl Rahner, is the Absolute Future. I believe that scientific discoveries during the last two centuries invite us to expand and intensify our hope for the coming of this Future. The startling picture of an expanding, still unfinished universe can provide a new sacramental setting for the lifting up of hearts.

In his hope-filled Closing Message of the Council (December 8, 1965), Pope Paul VI addressed, among other audiences, those whose lives are devoted to science: "Continue your search without tiring and without ever despairing of the truth," he said. "Happy are those who, while possessing the truth, search more earnestly for it in order to renew it, deepen it and transmit it to others. Happy also are those who, not having found it, are working toward it with a sincere heart. May they seek the light of tomorrow with the light of today until they reach the fullness of light."[3]

The Council's closing words are encouraging: "Never perhaps, thank God, has there been so clear a possibility as today of a deep understanding between real science and real faith, mutual servants of one another in the one truth. Do not stand in the way of this important meeting. Have confidence in faith, this great friend of intelligence. Enlighten yourselves with its light in order to take hold of truth, the whole truth."[4]

Gaudium et Spes, the Council's *Pastoral Constitution on the Church in the Modern World* (1965), had already expressed both the fruit and the promise of a new encounter of science with Christian faith and hope. After noting that the "scientific spirit exerts a new kind of impact" on culture and thought, the document makes two provocative claims that already express the importance of new scientific discoveries for theology and spirituality. The first is this: "The human race has passed from a rather static concept of reality to a more dynamic, evolutionary one. In consequence there has arisen a new series of problems.… calling for efforts of analysis and synthesis." [5] The second proposition, relying implicitly on the first, goes as follows: "A hope related to the end of time does not diminish the importance of intervening duties but rather undergirds the acquittal of them with fresh incentives." [21] The Council goes on to emphasize, in the spirit of Pope John XXIII's encyclical *Mater et Magistra*, that Christian hope does not lead to withdrawal from the world but instead to "bettering" [21] and "building" it. [34][5]

The two statements just mentioned provide a promising point of departure for implementing the Pope's and the Council's expectation of a rich future convergence of the seemingly separate worlds of science and Christian spirituality. For some of us the Council's words may seem so familiar by now that we fail to reflect deeply on their revolutionary theological, ethical and spiritual implications. Those present-day Christians for whom modernity seems essentially evil and spiritually regressive ignore or even dismiss the two claims just cited as a path toward the dead end of secularism. Why, they may ask, should we want to reconcile faith and theology with an evolutionary worldview? Evolution, after all, is an idea that strikes many Christians and Muslims as equivalent to materialism and atheism. It is an idea that seems dangerous theologically because it has been alloyed so often with shallow and even murderous "visions" of progress and social engineering. Didn't Hitler and Nazi eugenics, for example, appeal to Darwinian ideas? What exactly are the "fresh incentives" that Christian hope for final redemption gives to our "intervening duties" of "building the world?" And how does our hope for final redemption give added incentive to our moral decisions and duties here and now?

It is hard for me to read the Council's instructions without thinking of the Jesuit priest and geologist Pierre Teilhard de Chardin (1881-1955). In a variety of unpublished writings, especially in his posthumous books *The Human Phenomenon* (first English translation as *The Phenomenon of Man* in 1959) and *The Divine Milieu* (English translation, 1960), Teilhard had already anticipated the spirit of the Council and outlined ways to renew Christian thought and spirituality in the age of science.[6] Consequently, a closer look at Teilhard's own writings, although they were composed long before the Second Vatican Council, can still guide us as we reflect today on the Council's overtures to women and men of science.

There can be no doubt that Teilhard's ideas on faith and science are reflected visibly in *Gaudium et Spes*. The document clearly endorses, at least in principle, the brilliant Jesuit's call for transplanting Christian thought from its former cosmological setting in a static, pre-Copernican and pre-Darwinian worldview to a dynamic, evolutionary one. The renowned theologian Henri de Lubac, SJ, confirms this impression in his postconciliar remark that *Gaudium et Spes* expressed "precisely what Pére Teilhard sought to do."[7] The Teilhard scholar Robert Faricy, SJ, rightly refers to Teilhard's influence on the document as "a dominating one."[8] And it seems that a Teilhardian spirit of hope, renewal and "zest for living" informed the Council in other ways as well. So, fifty years later, as we reflect on the Council's potential influence, we would do well to examine more carefully than ever Teilhard's own efforts to frame a spiritual vision for the age of science.

During Teilhard's own lifetime, we may recall, Church censorship had prevented the publication of his innovative reflections on science and Christian faith. In 1962, the first year of the Council, the Vatican even sent a warning (*monitum*) to seminary and university teachers and officials advising them to "protect the minds, particularly of the youth, against the dangers presented by the works of Fr. Teilhard de Chardin and his followers."[9] Ostensibly, it was Teilhard's early and undeveloped attempts to reconcile original sin with evolution that had first alarmed his superiors. It seemed convenient to the latter, therefore, to let the brilliant young Jesuit scientist spend a quarter of a century virtually exiled in China, far from the European theater where he was already becoming too controversial. The long period in China, however, served only to nurture Teilhard's sense of the need to render Christianity relevant in terms of geology, evolutionary biology and cosmology's new sense of a still unfinished universe.

The Vatican's own censorship of Teilhard's writings is consistent with the fact that Church officials and theologians during Teilhard's lifetime were still highly skeptical of evolutionary science in general.[10] They were equally alarmed about world-affirming religious ideas such as those that Teilhard was building into his evolutionary vision. Remarkably, however, by the end of the Council, a mere decade after Teilhard's death, his Church had acknowledged the need to take the new evolutionary view of the world seriously and to redefine our Christian vocation accordingly. By the end of the Council Pope Paul VI is reported to have said: "Fr. Teilhard is an indispensable man for our times; his expression of faith is necessary for us!"[11]

Yet how many Catholics and how many theologians, seminarians, catechists and spiritual advisers have looked deeply enough into *Gaudium et Spes* to taste the Teilhardian "zest for living" that animates it.[12] Teilhard would certainly have applauded the Council's closing message that we are on the verge of "a deep understanding between real science and real faith, mutual servants of one another in the one truth."[13] But just how enthusiastic are most Catholics today about the Council's call for a fruitful, in-depth conversation between science and faith?

If Christian faith is to survive intellectual scrutiny in the age of science, as Teilhard had rightly come to see, it simply has to come to grips with science in general and evolution in particular. There can be little doubt that in our own day an honest embrace of scientific discoveries requires a theological readjustment and a reorientation of faith that seems too drastic for the majority of the world's Christians, including Catholics. In many ways we are still pre-Copernican or "fixist" in our religious and theological sensibilities. At times we tolerate evolution, but how often do we truly celebrate it as the backbone of a new spiritual vision? After Darwin and Big Bang physics have "called all in doubt," how many of us have learned how to lift up our hearts anew in the age of evolution? The fact that some noted scientific thinkers still try arbitrarily to merge evolution with philosophical materialism and atheism is not a good excuse for Christians to avoid the task of "analysis and synthesis" for which the Council calls.

Teilhard had died in 1955, but by the time of the Council his ideas on science and Christian faith had become familiar, either directly or indirectly, to at least some of the theologians and bishops at the Council. *The Phenomenon* was becoming a best seller in the area of religious thought for the Harper & Row publishing firm, so it was hard to ignore. *The Divine Milieu* appeared in French in 1957 and in English in 1960. Its spirituality of "divinizing" human action in the world is reflected in the Council's exhortation not to let our hopes for final redemption diminish the importance of "intervening duties" in our present existence.

Teilhard, of course, was not the only Catholic thinker to have made action and "building the world" an essential component of Christian spirituality and ethics, but the force of his integration of Christian faith with human effort and hope for the world's future is still unsurpassed. Moreover, it was Teilhard more than any other religious thinker of his time who brought the discoveries of the natural sciences to bear on the quest for a wholesome spirituality. Most remarkably, he made evolution the loom on which to weave any future Christian vision of hope. It was Teilhard who, even while digging ever deeper into the remote geological past, announced that the world "rests on the future as its sole support."[14] Only an evolutionary sense that something really big is taking shape up ahead can truly allow us to lift up our hearts in a way that will add incentive to our "intervening duties." By leaning toward the future, Christian spirituality after Galileo, Darwin and Big Bang cosmology can motivate our actions in a way that is fully consistent with the Christian doctrines of incarnation and redemption.

The Council seems to have embraced the Teilhardian view that what Christians may hope for is no longer reducible to the idea of the "harvesting" of human souls from an imperfect world. After Darwin and Einstein our sense of both cosmic and human destiny requires radical transformation. Spiritually speaking, we may look for the glory of God not only in the splendors or "designs" of nature but also in the story of a whole universe still coming into being. Science now allows Christians to respond to the threat of spiritual suffocation not only by lifting our eyes to the spatial immensity of the heavens but also, in the spirit of the apostle Paul, by hoping for the redemption and liberation of a not yet perfected universe.

Unfortunately, today, in my opinion, Catholic Christianity has largely forgotten, ignored, or failed to take spiritual advantage of the synthesis of science and faith in the future that provides at least part of the backdrop of *Gaudium et Spes*. Nor is there much interest in Teilhard's vision these days. In 1967 Archbishop Fulton J. Sheen wrote: "It is very likely that within fifty years when all the trivial, verbal disputes about the meaning of Teilhard's 'unfortunate' vocabulary will have died away or have taken a secondary place, Teilhard will appear like John of the Cross and St. Teresa of Avila, as the spiritual genius of the twentieth century."[15] I regret to say, however, that this prophecy has yet to be fulfilled. Almost half a century after Archbishop Sheen ventured his bold prediction, Teilhard's synthesis of Christianity and evolution remains largely unknown and undigested by most Catholics, including most of our theologians. Even those who have given notional assent to evolutionary science have been reluctant to think out carefully, as both Teilhard and the Council advise, what it really means that we have "passed from a rather static concept of reality to a more dynamic, evolutionary one." Has Catholic thought yet seriously begun to undertake what the Council refers to as the required new efforts of "analysis and synthesis"?

For many Catholics and other Christians, evolution, not unlike heliocentric cosmology in Donne's day, "calls all in doubt." When Teilhard began to undertake his own synthesis, his own Church discouraged such efforts, clinging instead to what Teilhard called the prescientific "fixist" (as distinct from evolutionary) picture of the universe. However, Vatican II has encouraged us to take up the work of analysis and synthesis regarding evolution that Teilhard had already begun. How many of us have done so? There is no doctrinal justification for avoiding the task of exploring what evolution implies for Christian faith and hope, but the fledgling efforts by a few Catholic thinkers to create a truly motivating evolutionary spirituality are marginal to the religious mentality of most Catholics. Evolution is now the central theme in the natural sciences, and in the intellectual world Darwin's ideas have never been more important than they are today. It is high time, then, that we take seriously the theological task enjoined by *Gaudium et Spes*. I can think of no better way to start than by reflecting critically once again on some of Teilhard's own efforts.

Teilhard's analysis and synthesis

To appreciate the constructive advice of *Gaudium et Spes* it may be helpful to reflect briefly here on several of Teilhard's pioneering ideas. To begin with, Teilhard noted often that evolution has profound theological significance simply by demonstrating that creation is still *unfinished*. If we would reflect carefully only on this single aspect of evolution, it would be theologically, spiritually and ethically momentous. Evolution means that the world is *still* coming into being. Each day the world is "raised a little farther out of nothingness."[16] After Darwin and Einstein the cosmos seems more open than ever before to a future of ongoing creation. In the cosmic journey something new and significant is always taking shape up ahead. Evolution, viewed theologically, implies that the universe is capable of *more being*. So our intervening duties must have something to do with our own contribution to the immense work of cosmic (and not just personal) transformation into something *more*.

If we had been present in the early universe and been able to survey it when it was still only an undifferentiated sea of radiation, how many of us would have predicted back then that the primordial plasma held the promise of eventually becoming stars, supernovae, carbon, life, mind, art, morality and the capacity to make promises? Yet even in its remotest origins all of these outcomes were already beginning undetectably to take shape "up ahead." Four billion years ago, when microorganisms first quietly emerged on Earth, the web of life was already beginning to weave itself into a *biosphere*. And after the biosphere appeared, an even newer sphere of mind and thought, of culture, morality, freedom, literacy, science and technology was already awaiting on the horizon of the future. The earth was beginning to clothe itself in something like a brain. The *noosphere*, a new envelope of *thought*, was beginning to take shape up ahead.[17] What, then, awaits our universe now that it has become conscious of itself in the recent appearance of human beings?

Only through increasingly intense *communion* of atoms, molecules, cells, and organisms with one another has the universe become *more* at every stage up to and including the present. So now that conscious persons have emerged in evolution it is only by way of interpersonal communion among these unique centers of reflection that *more being* can come about. And it is only mutual love, along with "a great hope held in common,"[18] that can bring these distinct personal centers together into a rich and differentiated unanimity "up ahead." For Teilhard, it is the function of Christian faith, hope and charity to foster this communion and thus contribute to the ongoing growth of the world. It is the sense that the world is still coming into being that can serve to lift up our hearts and give new incentive to our moral lives in this age of evolution.[19]

To give reasons for our hope Teilhard pointed to what he saw as a discernible direction in evolution and a general drift in cosmic process thus far. Evolution in the eyes of biologists may seem to resemble a drunken stagger, but overall the movement of the universe has been in the direction of increasing physical complexity, a point that even atheistic evolutionists must now accept. The cosmic process has passed from the relatively simple pre-atomic, atomic, and molecular stages to unicellular, multicellular, vertebrate, primate, and human forms of life. Overall, the long cosmic journey gives evidence of a measurable intensification of organized complexity. One can only wonder where this mysterious tendency toward complexification may lead in the future.

In any case, as visible matter has become more complex outwardly, the invisible interiority, centricity or "insideness" of things has also become more intense.[20] Having arrived at the level of human consciousness, there is no reason to assume that the universe's hunger for more being is now fully satisfied. The universe is still invited to become *more* by organizing itself inwardly and outwardly around an always new and higher Center. Ultimately this Center is the very God who in Christ has become fully incarnate in the universe and who still gathers the folds of the entire emergent Creation into his body.

For Teilhard, the incarnation of God in Christ continues to stir up the world. The entire cosmic process of creativity is always being called irreversibly and everlastingly into the life and redemptive compassion of God. Nothing in the story is ever lost or forgotten. Evolution means that creation is still happening, but that God is creating the world not *a retro*, that is, from out of the past, but *ab ante*, from up ahead.[21] All things are still being brought together in the Christ who is coming. As a devotee of St. Paul, Teilhard was convinced that what is *really* going on in evolution is that the "whole creation" is groaning for the renewal wrought by God in Christ through the power of the Holy Spirit.

Our spiritual hope, our "resting on the future," therefore, is simply the flowering of what has always been an anticipatory universe. Now, though us, the universe shows that it is still restless for further creation. Isn't it possible that something really big is still taking shape up ahead? And aren't our visions of the coming kingdom of God and the building up of the Body of Christ expressing through us the universe's own anticipation of more being? Nothing can lift up our hearts more fully than a sense that our intervening duties can contribute, no matter how small our individual offerings may seem, to the emergence of more being on the horizon of the cosmic future.

A sense that our lives really matter to the process of creation can in turn provide the incentive for a more robust ethical involvement in the world than if we think of ourselves as having been put here only to spin our moral wheels and thus prove ourselves virtuous enough to be harvested by the hereafter. The universe, as science has taught us, has always been ripening toward a new future long before human beings arrived on the scene. Today the Church of the prophets and Jesus should be the first to applaud science's great discovery that the universe is still pregnant with promise. It is this promise that can now prompt us to lift up our hearts as never before.

Teilhard was one of the first scientists to have noticed that the cosmos is a still-unfolding drama. He was among the first Christian thinkers to realize that the universe is not just a stage for the human drama, but that the stage is part of the drama. Human existence appears now in a whole new light. Our own lives are part of a larger creative cosmic process. Theologically this means that what we do with our lives is of consequence for the larger narrative of creation, as St. Paul had almost implied when he understood the redemption by Christ as something for which the whole of Creation has always been waiting (Rom 8:18-21). So the Council is justified on both scientific and biblical grounds in connecting our "intervening duties" to the final destiny of the universe in God. After Darwin and Einstein our action in the world matters because it contributes both to the deeper incarnation of God and to the redemptive gathering of the whole world, and not just human souls, into the being of Christ. The exhilarating Pauline intuition of a universe summed up in Christ (Col 1:13-20; Eph 1:9-10) matches up beautifully with our scientific understanding of a world struggling to become more. Reflecting on both the new scientific story of the universe and St. Paul's cosmic Christology, Teilhard notes how wondrously the doctrine of God's incarnation in Christ converges with the new scientific sense of a still-emerging universe.[22]

Finally, as Teilhard was aware, for many sincere scientifically educated people the universe has apparently outgrown their sense of God. It is encouraging to us, therefore, that even in the 1920's and 30's Teilhard was emphasizing that evolution and scientific cosmology provide the resources to give theology and spirituality an endlessly expansive understanding of God and a cosmic Christ worthy of our worship. So the Council's call for new "efforts of analysis and synthesis" can only be meant to include the need to ensure that we magnify our representations of God so that they always remain infinitely larger than science's expanding universe. In this and many other ways Teilhard's thought, whatever its limitations may be, still has an important role to play in our future implementation of the Council's encouragement of an ongoing transformation of faith and spirituality in this age of remarkable new scientific discoveries.

Dr. John F. Haught *is Senior Fellow, Science & Religion at the Woodstock Theological Center at Georgetown University in Washington, DC.*

DISCUSSION QUESTIONS

1. Does science challenge your faith in any way? If so, how do you respond to the challenge?
2. How would you contribute to the Council's call for new "analysis and synthesis" of the meaning of Christian faith now that human thought has moved toward an evolutionary understanding of the universe?
3. What is the meaning of Christ in the new age of evolution?

SUGGESTED READINGS

John F. Haught. *Making Sense of Evolution: Darwin, God, and the Drama of Life*. Louisville: Westminster John Knox Press, 2010.

Brian Swimme and Mary Evelyn Tucker. *The Journey of the Universe*. New Haven: Yale University Press, 2011.

Pierre Teilhard de Chardin. *The Divine Milieu*. New York: Harper & Row, 1960

NOTES

1. The expression is that of Teilhard de Chardin, *Activation of Energy*, trans. René Hague (New York: Harcourt Brace Jovanovich), 229-44.

2. Peter W. Atkins, *The 2nd Law: Energy, Chaos, and Form* (New York: Scientific American Books, 1994), 200.

3. Walter M. Abbott, Editor, *The Documents of Vatican II*

(New York: Guild Press, 1966), 730-71. Closing statement to "Men of Thought and Science," read by Paul Emile Cardinal Leger of Montreal, assisted by Antonio Cardinal Caggiano of Buenos Aires and Norman Cardinal Gilroy of Sydney, Australia.

4. Ibid.

5. Abbot, *Documents*, 203-4; 218; 233.

6. Pierre Teilhard de Chardin, *The Human Phenomenon*, trans. Sarah Appleton-Weber (Portland, Oregon: Sussex Academic Press, 1999); Pierre Teilhard de Chardin, *The Divine Milieu* (New York: Harper & Row, 1960).

7. Henri de Lubac, SJ, *The Eternal Feminine: A Study of the Text of Teilhard de Chardin* (London: Collins, 1971), 136, cited by David Lane, *The Phenomenon of Teilhard: Prophet for a New Age* (Macon GA: Mercer University Press, 1996), 88.

8. Robert Faricy, SJ, *All Things in Christ: Teilhard de Chardin's Spirituality* (London: Fount Paperbacks, 1981), 52 (cited by David Lane, *The Phenomenon of Teilhard*).

9. "Warning Considering the Writings of Father Teilhard de Chardin," Sacred Congregation of the Holy Office, June 30, 1962.

10. For an excellent summary of official Catholic aversion to evolution between the wars see Don O'Leary, *Roman Catholicism and Modern Science* (New York: Continuum, 2006), 129-66.

11. Cited by Wayne Kraft, *The Relevance of Teilhard* (Notre Dame IN: Fides), 29.

12. *Teilhard, Activation of Energy*, 229-44.

13. Abbott, *Documents*, 731.

14. Teilhard, *Activation of Energy*, 239.

15. Fulton J. Sheen, *Footsteps in a Darkened Forest* (New York: Meredith, 1967), 73.

16. Pierre Teilhard de Chardin, *The Prayer of the Universe*, trans. René Hague (New York: Harper & Row, 1973), 121.

17. Teilhard, *The Human Phenomenon*, 122-25 and *passim*.

18. Pierre Teilhard de Chardin, *The Future of Man*, trans. Norman Denny (New York: Harper Colophon Books, 1964), 75.

19. For a fuller development of all these themes see Teilhard, *The Human Phenomenon*.

20. Teilhard, *The Human Phenomenon*, 27, 207.

21. Pierre Teilhard de Chardin, *Christianity and Evolution*, trans. René Hague (New York: Harcourt Brace & Co., 1969), 240.

22. Pierre Teilhard de Chardin, *Human Energy*, trans. J. M. Cohen (New York: Harvest Books/Harcourt Brace Jovanovich, 1962), 82-102.

Conclusion

Holiness in the Future, Holiness as Future

Michael W. Higgins

Lawrence Cunningham has argued that "Vatican II was more centrally concerned, because of its fundamentally pastoral orientation, with the ordinary spiritual development of ordinary Christians than any council in history."[1] Not surprisingly, then, the chapter in *Lumen Gentium* titled "The Universal Call to Holiness" says it all, or at least explains the motif of holiness as a thread that winds itself throughout several of the documents of the Council. Holiness is serious stuff.

Allow me to identify what I consider *five* distinct strands that we can detect in post-conciliar spirituality.

First, *the spirituality of the wounded*, the most popular exposition of which we can find in *The Wounded Healer*, an early work by the Dutch priest-psychologist Henri J.M. Nouwen. He realized that the loneliness and alienation often experienced by the healing professionals, and most especially those who are ministers of the spirit, could be a precious gift.

A deep understanding of their own pains, however, makes it possible for them to convert their weakness into strength and to offer their own experience as a source of healing to those confounded by their own spiritual confusion and the oppressive miasma of seemingly meaningless suffering. Nouwen's tone in this work as well as in his subsequent writing (he authored forty books by the time of his death in 1996) was honest without being ostentatious; he maintained a syllogistic but not constrictive logic in his writing, and he wrote to revel and not conceal God's encompassing love.

More than anything, Nouwen was committed to shaping a voice for the wounded—the physically handicapped and mentally challenged, the socially marginalized and politically persecuted, the lonely and sexually oppressed/repressed.

But a *spiritually of the wounded* isn't exclusively Nouwen territory. Although he made the title "wounded healer" his own in 1972, he was quick to acknowledge those whose ministry with the wounded, healers or otherwise, was of long-standing and estimate quality. And none perhaps fit into this category more fully than his European eulogist, the Canadian philosopher, spiritual writer, activist, and co-founder of L'Arche, Jean Vanier. Founded during the Second Vatican Council, L'Arche is a ministry to the handicapped that has global outreach. Vanier was persuaded that the broken of mind and body have a unique ministry that must not be ignored. He labored to create an environment in which the fractured, the shattered, and the forsaken can find healing and where healers, too, are healed. Vanier's call to community is not a romantic's fantasy. To love is messy, requires a naked openness, exposes our most acute vulnerabilities, makes no apologies in its demands. The intellectually challenged are needy, relentless, and importunate, feeling wildly, loving unconditionally. They are the principal teachers. The caregivers come to value them less as dependents and more as vessels of light. They teach us the way of the heart.

Vanier's *spirituality of the wounded* is a spirituality enmeshed in the world of broken bodies, broken minds, and broken spirits. But Vanier knows that to break open the "plague of cerebration," a term Thomas Merton used when describing the malaise that afflicts the fictional world of the French-Algerian existentialist novelist Albert Camus, a plague that poisons our own contemporary culture, we must allow "the wounded" to heal our wounds, allow the maimed to touch our invisible scars of heart and mind. In short, we must be vulnerable as they are vulnerable. The "other" becomes a gift to us.

The second strand of spirituality is directly identifiable with this same Thomas Merton, a Trappist monk, poet, literary essayist, spiritual writer, and social critic who spent a lifetime defining a *spirituality of the monastic cell*, and in doing so appealed to those both inside and outside the cloister. Merton resolved to bring the wisdom of the desert to the inhabitants of plaza and condominium, the sage counsels of the ancient holy ones to the struggling masses of the modern metropolis. He anticipated the Second Vatican

Council's commitment to *ressourcement*, going back to the primitive sources that feed our thought and spirituality; he restored the special place of the early Cistercians in the history of Christian spirituality, recovered their insights for modernity, and mined the rich ground of the early contemplatives to fashion a spirituality for a new age. The Council's outpouring of new energy and vivifying insights owes much to the decades of work done by Merton and others like Dom Jean Leclerq to reclaim the learning and relevance of medieval culture for our time.

Merton made monasticism palatable for his contemporaries. But he wasn't the only one to do so. Benedictine Dom John Main, a one-time professor of international jurisprudence at Dublin's Trinity College, sought in his many books and lectures to teach a form of meditation that is accessible to those outside the cloisters. Main and his Oxford-trained disciple and heir to the mantle of his leadership in Christian Meditation, Lawrence Freeman, ensure that the curative power of wordless prayer and silence are now our common property.

It has become quite possible to find a "professional prayer-smith" as much out of the monastery as in. These exclaustrated "monks"—lay and sometimes not even Catholic—have become a remarkable spiritual phenomenon. Their most outstanding exemplar is the best-selling Benedictine oblate, poet, and American spiritual writer, Kathleen Norris. In her uniquely crafted memoir/reflection compendia, *The Cloister Walk* (1996) and *Amazing Grace: A Vocabulary of Faith* (1998), Norris takes the reader through a liturgical cycle that draws on the rich experience of being human. She leaves out nothing. *Everything is a means of grace.*

The *spirituality of the Ignatian way* is the third strand and is both rigorously apostolic and contemplative. It is first and foremost grounded in the spiritual life of St. Ignatius of Loyola himself.

For centuries, Ignatian spirituality was almost exclusively identified with Jesuit spirituality: it was their possession. And then a revolution occurred.

From 1965 on, just after conclusion of the Second Vatican Council, the North American Jesuit masters of novices were having their formal meetings and realized that in keeping with the Council's wish for *ressourcement* they needed to go back to the original Jesuit sources and restore the one-to-one focus of the Spiritual Exercises, the cornerstone of Jesuit identity.

In addition, this very same Jesuit spirituality is a spirituality of right knowing and of making things just. Richly expanded as a ministry to non-Jesuit clerics, religious sisters, Catholic laity and now non-Catholics and even non-Christians in search of a depth experience of God, the spirituality of the Ignatian way does not so much proscribe experience, which many pre-conciliar spiritualities were inclined to do, as much as it invites one to sift and gauge the true measure of one's affective life. It also calls one to justice; it is not a cocooned spirituality, insular, self-referential and secure.

But there are other spiritual ways as well that also unite a passion for justice with the cultivation of a deep prayer life as we see with the fourth strand, a *spirituality of poverty and protest.* Perhaps no more clear and more lasting an example of this mode of Christian witness can be found than the Catholic Worker movement, the brainchild of activist and journalist Dorothy Day and worker-philosopher Peter Maurin. Although the Catholic Workers long pre-dated the Council chronologically, the spirit of the Council invigorated, validated and emboldened their ministry to "society's least."

As Roberto Goizueta observed in his chapter on the Council letter addressed to the poor, sick and suffering, "the very existence of the wounded in our midst is so terrifying that we must eradicate them or, at least, hide them from view…so that we don't have to see them…and their uncomfortable wounds." And out of that profound societal tension to *either* eliminate the poor from our view *or* take them seriously as the vehicle of our own redemption were born many of the movements, congregations and secular institutes that constitute the fifth and final strand—*the spirituality of resistance or restoration.*

Although some of these ecclesial movements, etc., predate the Second Vatican Council, all of them have greatly prospered in numbers, influence, and power during the reign of John Paul II. These movements—although they are largely lay in composition, many of them have clerics specifically ordained to serve their membership—include the highly influential Opus Dei (a personal prelature whose founder Josémaría Escrivá de Balaguer has been canonized by John Paul II), Communion and Liberation, the Neocatechumenate, the Focolare, Faith, Miles Jesu, and many others. Most of them are conservative, pietistic, scrupulously loyal to the Supreme Pontiff, well-versed in the laws and traditions of the Church, intelligent, sincere, and tireless in expending their energies in the interests of institutional Catholicism. Some are more prophetic in their origins and thrust, like the San Egidio Community in Rome, whose notion of discipleship not only involves feeding the hungry and clothing the naked but also working as peacemakers, reconciling enemies and ameliorating the damage of social and civil discord.

Any spirituality of resistance or restoration by its nature asks the fundamental questions: Who are the poor and where do we stand in relation to them? How we answer the question depends on whether we are inclined to see our spirituality as a mode of prophetic defiance or creative restoration. If it is the latter, then we are likely to be engaged in a recovery of that sense of the transcendent, of the numinous, that has been tragically lost following what has been perceived as the ravaging excesses of the Council's liturgical reforms. In addition, such a spirituality is likely to be firmly situated within an established tradition of spirituality that is fully cognizant of the conventions and forms of piety that are historically conditioned yet desirous of their imaginative recovery or reinstatement. A spirituality with an emphasis on restoration will be characterized by a close affinity with spiritual luminaries of the past and with a visceral fidelity to the institutional Church and its hierarchy.

A genuine spirituality of resistance, however, grounded in a love both for justice and for the contemplative dimension, will have little time for the easy spiritualities that are so effortlessly marketed in Western culture as the next phase in self-fulfillment. It is also a spirituality focused on the Spirit's surprising unfolding and not on the Spirit's recreating the old order, working for a new understanding and not for restitution of received ways.

As Diana Hayes notes in her chapter on the Council's letter to women, longing for the righting of an understanding of women that has been for centuries truncated if not overtly discriminatory, "we cannot go back because the past is just that, it is gone, over with. Too much has changed within church and society. Nostalgia is fine in its place but our emphasis should be on preparing for the future. Much has been accomplished but much more needs to be done for the fullness of the vision of Vatican II to be realized."

A spirituality that is communal, historical, theological, with justice as part of its very definition, is a spirituality best poised to thrive in the new century, a spirituality of resistance that is not dismissive of the past, hampered by a crippling nostalgia or self-occupied and insular.

Although it is a cliché to say that times are desperate, for the Church they clearly are. The acute instances of institutional dysfunction cannot be gainsaid and to the credit of the various sections of the Church—progressive, reactionary, conservative and liberal (and admittedly these categories are all inadequate in defining the complex array of convictions and attitudes ascribed to them)—all have acknowledged the malaise that has overcome the *ecclesia*—or at least a major part of its current historical iteration.

Struggles over governance, canonical and magisterial prerogatives, the obligations of the theologian in and to the believing community, the right exercise by the episcopacy of a nurturing and not censorious oversight, the tensions around collegiality and subsidiarity in the larger ecclesiastical context, and the credibility of authority itself—all these visible and vexatious marks of discord are in part the legacy of the Council, a reminder that the process of appropriation, of reception, is a long and torturous one.

Rather than give in to despair—the temptation is ever-present —or to recrimination—an easy enough and natural response to those forces and persons who threaten to sunder what we most treasure—we should do what English priest-poet and spiritual writer Daniel O'Leary calls on us to do: recover the beauty of the word, expel the dullness of prose from our discourse, and recall Hans Urs von Balthasar's admonition that what a prophet has to say can never be said in prose.[2]

And there was one who could write as a poet while at the same time being a scientist, a paleontologist with a mystic's sensibility. John Haught makes it clear in his chapter on the Council's letter to scientists that re-connecting with the vision of Pierre Teilhard de Chardin, the Jesuit thinker who died just four years before John XXIII announced his intention to convoke a council, is a salutary challenge, a *kairos* moment. Teilhard, Haught argues, knew that "evolution and scientific cosmology provide the resources to give theology and spirituality an endlessly expansive understanding of God and a cosmic Christ worthy of our worship."

And that is precisely what we need fifty years after the Council's opening: "an endlessly expansive understanding of God" and with it a holiness that is poetic, visionary, sapiential and incarnational—a holiness embedded in the beautiful and prophetic—a holiness *of* the Council and a holiness *for* the future.

*Parts of this concluding chapter are a distillation of a more detailed treatment that I made in "Spiritual in Essence and Form" in *Power and Peril: the Catholic Church at the Crossroads* by Michael W. Higgins and Douglas R. Letson (Toronto: HarperCollins, 2002) and in "Jesuit as Spiritual Director" in *The Jesuit Mystique* by Michael W. Higgins and Douglas R. Letson (London: Harper-Collins, 1995).

Dr. Michael W. Higgins *is Vice President for Mission and Catholic Identity and Professor of Religious Studies at Sacred Heart University in Fairfield, CT.*

NOTES

1. Lawrence S. Cunningham, "Vatican II and Spirituality," *The New Westminister Dictionary of Christian Spirituality*, edited by Philip Sheldrake (Louisville: WJK Press, 2005), 630.

2. Daniel O' Leary, "Power of Words," *The Tablet*, April 7, 2012, 10.